BOMBAY DUCKS

BOMBAY DUCKS

AN ACCOUNT OF SOME OF THE EVERY-DAY BIRDS AND BEASTS FOUND IN A NATURALIST'S ELDORADO

DOUGLAS DEWAR

GYAN

Published by

GYAN

Gyan Publishing House
5, Ansari Road
Daryaganj, New Delhi-110002
Phone: 011-47034999, 9811692060
E-mail: books@gyanbooks.com

Distribution Network
gyanbooks.com
India, USA, Canada, UK, Australia

ISBN: 978-93-3300-357-5 (PB)

First Published, 1906

2nd Impression 2025

Printed at: Gyan Press, Delhi.

BOMBAY DUCKS
Author: DOUGLAS DEWAR

BOMBAY DUCKS

BY THE SAME AUTHOR

ANIMALS OF NO IMPORTANCE

THE INDIAN CROW: HIS BOOK

THE KING CROW

BOMBAY DUCKS

AN ACCOUNT OF SOME OF THE EVERY-DAY BIRDS AND BEASTS FOUND IN A NATURALIST'S ELDORADO

BY DOUGLAS DEWAR, F.Z.S., I.C.S.

WITH NUMEROUS ILLUSTRATIONS FROM PHOTOGRAPHS OF LIVING BIRDS BY CAPTAIN F. D. S. FAYRER, I.M.S.

LONDON JOHN LANE THE BODLEY HEAD
NEW YORK JOHN LANE COMPANY MDCCCCVI

PREFACE

SOME apology is perhaps necessary for the title of this book, since the "Ducks" herein dealt with belong not to the quack-quack tribe.

"Bombay Ducks" is a time-honoured Anglo-Indian expression.

In the palmy days of the East India Company, when the now-barren pagoda-tree showered its fruits upon all who shook it, the European residents of the Western Presidency were known as Bombay Ducks to distinguish them from Bengal Qui-his and Madras Mulls.

In very early times "Ducks" was spelt "Duckys" and is probably a corruption of the Latin *duces* = leaders or "bosses."

Dwellers in Bombay are no longer called ducks, nevertheless the expression Bombay Ducks or Bombay Duck still survives.

It now denotes (I know not why) brittle pieces of sun-dried fish which are eaten with curry in South India.

It seems to me that the animals dealt with in this volume, all of which are to be found on the "Bombay side," have at least an equal right with pieces of dried fish to be called "Bombay Ducks."

The illustrations are reproductions of photographs of living birds taken by Captain R. S. F. Fayrer, I.M.S.

Efforts have been made to produce, not so much a series of pretty pictures as a number of likenesses that will assist people to identify the originals when they meet them in the flesh.

How far the photographer has been successful every reader must judge for himself; but only those who have tried to photograph living birds will be able fully to appreciate the value of Captain Fayrer's work.

D. D.

These "Ducks" first made themselves heard in one or other of the following newspapers:—*The Times of India*, *The Madras Mail*, *The Indian Daily Telegraph*, *The Morning Post of India*.

Since some have found their voices not unpleasant, they have been allowed a second quack.

CONTENTS

ILLUSTRATIONS

BOMBAY DUCKS

"And all the jungle laughed with nesting songs,
And all the thickets rustled with small life
Of lizard, bee, beetle, and creeping things
Pleased at the spring time. In the mango sprays
The sun-birds flashed; alone at his green forge
Toiled the loud coppersmith; bee-eaters hawked,
Chasing purple butterflies; beneath
Striped squirrels raced; the mynas perked and picked,
The seven sisters chattered in the thorn,
The pied fish-tiger hung above the pool,
The egrets stalked among the buffaloes,
The kites sailed circles in the golden air;
About the painted temple peacocks flew."

The Light of Asia.

BOMBAY DUCKS

DOVES

DOVES are birds for which I entertain the greatest respect. They remind me of certain urchins who were my companions at a dame's school to which I was sent for the sins of my early youth. Notwithstanding the fact that the aforesaid urchins were the originators of all mischief, the respectable ladies in authority were in the habit of holding them up as models to be copied by the rest of the school. Those boys were not hypocrites, they did not falsely pretend innocence; there was no need for them to do so. Fortune was always kind to them: she never allowed them to commit the fatal crime of being found out. Thus they passed their early schooldays chuckling at the sweet simplicity of the dames to whose care they had been confided. So it is with doves. Without conscious efforts, these birds have succeeded in persuading mankind that they are paragons of virtue.

"The whole life and being of the dove," wrote Dr.

Masius, "is a pleasing idyl. They are chaste, gentle, unsuspecting, full of tender affection, and deserve above all others the epithet of 'the pious birds.' Without guile, like doves, it is said in the Bible. Without guile and free from anger, suffering all, even death, and not once uttering a cry of pain, what other animal may be compared to them?

"The dove alone, according to the ancients, is destitute of gall; and in a hundred popular rhymes and love-songs, as well as in the metaphors of the medieval wandering preachers, the praise of her innocence resounds."

This may be taken as a fair statement of popular opinion of the dove. Some people go further. Thus dear old Eliza Cook says: "Linnets teach us how to love, and ring-doves how to pray." Now I do not wish to poke fun at that estimable and well-meaning lady, but I am constrained to say that it is unfortunate that she did not study the ways of the dove a little before penning the above line. Had she but invested eighteenpence in one of the cooing community, she might have said of them: "They teach us how to swear." But then, of course, the question would arise, do men need to be taught that accomplishment? I am inclined to think that swearers, like poets, are born, not made.

How delightful is the idea that doves are "free from anger!" I once knew a dove which was in a rage for a whole week because it had been transferred from one cage to another. It did not approve of the style of architecture of its new habitation, so sat, for the space of one week, with ruffled feathers looking like a barn-door fowl about to die. Not content with this, it swore at every one who went near it.

Those who really believe that doves are incapable of anger should make a point of seeing a couple of them mobbing a tree-pie that has just breakfasted off their eggs. Let me not be mistaken. I am not finding fault with the doves. I hold that their anger is perfectly justified under such circumstances.

The biblical doctrine of turning the unsmitten cheek to the smiter does not apply to them. Since, however, they act just as any other little bird would do under similar circumstances, it is obviously incorrect to speak of them alone as "free from anger." It gives one an altogether false idea of the character of the dove. That worthy bird is ever ready to take the law into its own hands. Then, again, I have never been able to discover any piety about the dove. Complacency it undoubtedly possesses, the complacency of the self-made man. But this surely is not piety!

"How," remarks Phil Robinson, who goes to the opposite extreme and is very severe on doves, "if the doves could read English poetry, would they put their tongues in their cheeks and wink at each other, and how the worse conditioned of them would explode with laughter!" He maintains that doves have acquired their spurious reputation for saintliness because they make such a fuss, such an amount of cooing over their love affairs. To this must, I think, be added the general butter-will-not-melt-in-my-mouth appearance of the bird. A dove looks so defenceless; but it cannot be so helpless as it appears, otherwise the species would long ago have become extinct.

When doves are not cooing they usually sit half asleep on a telegraph wire, exposed to the gaze of every bird of prey in the vicinity; yet I have never seen a dove carried off by any of the pirates of the air. How is this? It is not that doves are inedible; dove pie is not at all a bad dish. I speak as one having authority, although I do so with bated breath, for fear of disturbing in their graves Byron, Prior, Shelley, Thomson, and all the other admirers of the dove. I repeat, I speak as one with authority, for I was once sent to an arid and inhospitable district in India where butchers and bakers were non-existent and *shikar* there was none.

I was therefore restricted to a diet of *chapatti* and dove, varied occasionally by a pea-chick, marked down and shot sleeping after the shades of night had fallen, so as not to offend the susceptibilities of the unsophisticated villager. In some parts of India the peacock is accounted sacred. Dove's flesh is a trifle insipid, but in every way preferable to *dâk* bungalow fowl, while young pea-chick is equal to Christmas turkey, but an old peacock is the dickens!

Doves are in many ways beautiful birds, but their beauty is not appreciated in India. In the first place, they are to us common, everyday creatures, and human nature is so constituted that it is unable to admire any object which it sees daily. Then doves, as a rule, are not showy. To quote "Eha": "They rarely carry any meretricious ornament, such as crests, or trains, or fancy plumes, but they are all beautiful, and some of them

SPOTTED DOVE

exquisitely lovely. Yet their loveliness is not that of golden orioles and kingfishers, but rather of clouds and distant hills and soft sunsets."

There is, however, one marked exception, and that is the bronze-winged dove (*Chalcophaps indica*). This is a perfect rainbow of colour, and a full description of it would occupy half a page. It must suffice that, as it flashes through a shady glade, it appears to be a thing, now of emerald-green, now of coppery bronze. It is found only in the well-wooded parts of the country. The commonest species of dove in India is the spotted dove (*Turtur suratensis*). Looked at from a distance, it appears a plain, dingy, reddish-brown bird. Closer inspection reveals a russet-brown head and neck, set off by a black tippet spotted with white. The tail and wings are brownish with rufous spots. Its black-and-white cape suffices to distinguish it from all other kinds of dove. The ringdove (*Turtur risorius*) is also a bird seen all over India. It is grey with a collar composed of a broad black band, bordered on each side by a narrow white one. It has a treble note *co-co-coo.*

Doves are strict vegetarians, and they subsist chiefly upon grain. They seem to breed all the year round, and considering the number of the birds existing in India, one comes across remarkably few nests. It is not that doves take extraordinary precautions to conceal their nurseries. They build by preference in a *babul* tree, which affords remarkably little cover. The nest escapes detection because it is not of strictly orthodox construction. Phil Robinson compares it to a heap of spillikins. According to him, if you would make an imitation dove's nest you have only to upset half a box of matches. "As a boy," he writes, "I have sometimes discovered the nest *by seeing the eggs in it from below!* It is a mere skeleton, a network, and in its way a miracle. In fact, it is not a nest at all." This, of course, is not the poet's idea of the nest. The bard pictures it as a delightfully woven structure, beautifully lined with feathers and down. Saith Keats:—

"Warm as a dove's nest among summer trees."

A draughtier abode than a dove's nest it would be difficult to imagine. To the naturalist, the ghost of a nest constructed by the dove is most interesting. It possibly throws some light on the origin of the wonderful nest-building instinct. How this instinct arose is to me one of the most difficult problems in natural history. The primitive bird undoubtedly laid its eggs on the ground—on the sand, or among rocks and stones.

Then some bird learned to lay them in the grass. Next, perhaps, some species deposited them on a dense shrub. Eggs so laid would be apt to slip down and be lost, so any tendency to make a surface for the eggs by laying a few sticks upon the bush would be to preserve by the action of natural selection. By degrees the instinct must have developed until we eventually arrive at the wonderful nest of the weaver bird.

This is all pure conjecture, but it seems to me that the nest-building instinct must have originated in some such manner. Perhaps the dove has kept to the methods of its early ancestors, while most of the other birds have improved upon them. There is much to be said in favour of the dove's method, for, other things being equal, the more pronounced the structure of the nest, the more conspicuous is it likely to be. In this Spartan nursery the dove lays two white eggs. Seen from below, they may be mistaken for the sky, but from above, they are presumably somewhat conspicuous. The owners of the nest, however, keep a close watch over the nest, and doves, in spite of their reputed gentleness, are quite able to drive off most adversaries.

One reads much about the protective colouration of birds' eggs, and many are doubtless coloured so as to be inconspicuous in the nest or place where they are laid. But it seems to me that the theory of protective colouration is usually carried too far. This is a subject to which I shall have occasion to again and again refer. When there are eggs in the nest most birds keep near it, and show themselves ready to fight any would-be thieves. It is, I believe, upon this characteristic of the owners of the nest, rather than the colouring of the eggs, that the protection of these latter depends. Few birds will dare to rob the nest of even a smaller bird if the owner shows that he means fight. Under such circumstances a great kite will fly ignominiously from a pair of diminutive king-crows. An ounce of good solid pugnacity is a more useful weapon in the struggle for existence than many pounds of protective colouring.

THE OCCUPATIONS OF ANIMALS

IT is pleasant to recline in the shade of a stately deodar with no company but one's thoughts, and thus to gaze at the purple wreaths of tobacco smoke as they ascend towards the blue heavens. It is sweet to experience the cool Himalayan breeze direct from the snowy mountains that fill the northern landscape. It is very soothing to listen to the sleepy hum of the insects, and to watch the little birds as they flit from branch to branch of the neighbouring trees. How desperately busy these tiny feathered creatures seem to be! They move as though their life were a race against time. Yet they have nothing to do save seek their food, which abounds on all sides. As I contemplate them I ask myself the old, old question, How is it that birds and beasts manage to pass through life without succumbing to ennui, or, at least, without being bored nearly to death? To me the life of a bird is incomprehensible, but then so is that of a *chaprassi*. I admit that I am at present doing nothing; but I shall soon grow weary of this. '*Dolce far niente*' for a short time.

Animals, as a rule, do not loaf; it is not thus that they solve the problem. Loafing is an art which but few living creatures understand. Lizards, crocodiles, paddy birds, and *chaprassis* are the greatest authorities on the subject. Animals have acquired the knack of making much ado about nothing; they have learned to be very busy without doing anything. This accomplishment obviously differs from that of loafing. It is one which animals have brought to perfection, and of which many human beings—chiefly women—are very able exponents.

There is overhead a wasp busy exploring the holes in the trunk of a tree. Why he does this he probably does not know; he has no time to stop and think. He is quite content to explore away as though his life depended upon it. Five times within the last six minutes he has minutely inspected every portion of the same hole. All this labour is useless in a sense; without it, however, the wasp would in all probability die of ennui. The wasp is not an isolated case.

Most animals are experts at frittering away time; they spend much of their lives in actively doing nothing. Watch a canary in a cage. He hops backwards and forwards, between two perches, as though he was paid by the distance for doing so.

Look at a butterfly. It leads an aimless existence, nevertheless it is always busy. A bee probably visits twenty times as many flowers in the day as a butterfly; for all that the butterfly is always on the move.

When speaking of the swift in my volume, "Animals of no Importance," I noticed how long that bird took to find the materials for its nest, how it went afar to seek that which was at hand. This, although the result of stupidity, is doubtless a blessing to the bird. Nest-building affords great pleasure to it—the more protracted the amusement, the better for the architect.

The squirrel labours from early morn till late eve laying up a store of nuts. When one storehouse is full the industrious animal opens another, and then proceeds to forget the existence of the first!

Go to the running stream and watch the kingfisher at work. He does not select a suitable place and keep to it; he flies from rock to rock and continually makes excursions up and down the river, and is thus enabled to spend the whole of the day in fishing and yet not overeat himself.

It may be asked, How do sessile animals solve the problem? The sea-squirt, the sponge, and the barnacle are non-locomotive, and hence they cannot fritter away their time as a butterfly does. I reply, that for these degenerate creatures, sans eyes, sans teeth, sans everything, there is no problem to solve. Sessile animals are, to all intents and purposes, plants; they are creatures devoid of feeling. An oyster has no more soul than a dandelion.

To return to the higher animals. The search for food undoubtedly occupies a very large portion of their day, even if they waste no time. It is not an uncommon thing to find over one thousand seeds in the crop of a granivorous bird. Suppose such a creature is able to find and swallow two hundred seeds in an hour, then the eating of a thousand represents five hours' solid work. Insectivorous birds, such as wagtails, must eat several hundreds of insects in a day. Animals that live upon bigger game, which cannot be caught without much effort, no doubt often find that the day is none too long to enable them to obtain a sufficient meal.

It is a merciful provision of nature that herbivorous animals, whose food is lying waiting for them on all sides, have to eat a terrific quantity in order to satisfy their hunger, otherwise such creatures would surely soon grow weary of life. Animals spend much time in sleep. The lower the development of the brain, the more repose its possessor seems to need.

Some one has said that of the twenty-four hours a wise man requires to sleep seven, a woman eight, a child nine, and an idiot ten. The lower animals probably slumber from twelve to fourteen hours a day. Most of them sleep from sunset to dawn, while almost every animal enjoys a prolonged rest during the heat of the day in the warmer weather.

Only yesterday I was watching a wagtail hunting for insects amid the stones of a mountain stream. There was no beating about the bush with him; he meant business, and most methodical was his search. Then, quite suddenly, into his downy shoulders went his head, while one leg was retracted into his ruffled feathers, and, then and there, on a stone in midstream, he took forty winks. Presently he roused himself as suddenly and renewed the hunt.

Every one must have noticed at the Zoological Gardens that, except at feeding-time, the majority of the animals are asleep. Of course, I am aware that such animals do not live natural or healthy lives, and I

PIED WAGTAIL

only allude to them to show what animals are capable of in the way of sleep.

Lastly, animals spend no inconsiderable portion of the day in play. The play of animals is too big a subject to be discussed at the tail end of an essay. It must suffice that nearly all the higher animals indulge in play; some go as far as to play regular games.

The life of an animal bears the same relation to that of a human being as an anthem does to a polemic oration. The anthem is made up of one short paragraph; the speech is replete with facts and figures. The delivery of each may occupy the same time. In the former, two or three phrases are sung and resung; in the latter, weighty sentences follow in rapid succession, one upon the other.

It may be said that, if such be the case, if animals have thus to drag out their lives, they cannot be happy. This I deny. Animals are not aware of the fact that they are frittering away their lives, that they do much useless work. The singing of an anthem causes as much pleasure to the chorister as the delivery of a great speech to the orator.

I took out my pony this morning. She had not left her stable for several days, except for walking exercise. Was she bored by her long sojourn in the stable? Not in the least. She seemed very loath to leave it. During the whole of the outward journey she was making attempts to turn homewards, and when at last her desire was realized, her pace was visibly accelerated.

The dog forms an exception. No doubt he does get tired of doing nothing. The piteous wail of a hound chained to his kennel affords proof of this. If further evidence be demanded, there are the unmistakable signs of pleasure exhibited by a dog when his master picks up hat and stick. Man has taken away from the dog his chief occupation, and often gives him little or nothing to do in return. The same, indeed, applies to other domestic animals, but they show no signs of ennui. Between them and the dog there is a difference. The latter has become the friend and companion of man, and in consequence has acquired a little of his master's restless spirit. The dog, therefore, stands upon a plane above that occupied by the rest of the lower animals.

GREEN PARROTS

GREEN parrots bear living testimony to the truth of the Psalmist's complaint that the wicked flourish like the green bay tree. A more aggressively flourishing tribe of wicked birds it would be difficult to imagine. Green parrots live on the fat of the land, and let all the world know it. Nevertheless, their sins do not go altogether unpunished. A very considerable portion of the parrot folk are condemned to lifelong imprisonment in little metal cages, which, when hung out in the sunshine, are as hot as——well, as a tropical country can be! Such an existence, however, does not appear to depress a parrot.

There is something sleek and self-satisfied about the bird which no amount of affliction can obliterate. I have never seen a "pretty Poll" who has not the complaisant air of a self-made man. Some human beings have a parrot-like expression. Such individuals appear to be proud of the fact, for they invariably hold a very good opinion of themselves. And it is but fair to them to add that, in most cases, this opinion is justified. A man with a parrot-like face is usually a good fellow.

Even the self-satisfaction of the green parrot is not without justification; the bird is beautiful. The common form, which haunts most of our compounds in India, is known to men of science as the rose-ringed paroquet, or *Palæornis torquatus*. The grass-green plumage of this species must be familiar to every one in England, for the bird is on sale in every fancier's shop. The two sexes do not wear exactly similar plumage. The male has a rose-coloured collar and a black necktie, while his wife has, by way of a collar, to put up with an emerald-green ring round her neck, and, being a mere woman, is obliged to go through life without the luxury of a necktie.

If there be anything in phrenology, the green parrot must have the bump of destructiveness very largely developed. The bird is never so happy as when it is destroying the crop sown by some poor *raiyat;* and, since parrots are restrained by neither law nor a moral sense, there is no hindrance to their self-indulgence, except the small boys who are told off to watch the crops; but these urchins only serve to add zest to parrot existence.

Polly's larcenies would lose half their charm had not the thief the pleasure of dodging the ill-aimed stones of the small watchmen. The methods of green parrots are copied from those of Indian jungle folk, or perhaps the converse is the case. Of this each man must judge for himself. It is for me but to state the sober fact that if an unsophisticated villager desires the wherewithal to build him a house, and if the aforesaid villager lives in the neighbourhood of a "reserved forest," he forthwith betakes himself into the said forest and proceeds to cut down the twelve most promising saplings upon which he can lay his axe.

THE ROSE-RINGED PARAKEET

In the same way, when a flock of green parrots invades a wheat field, each bird does not confine its depredations to one blade of corn until it is devoured. That would be very poor sport. Every man, woman, and child parrot selects a grain-laden stalk and, having enjoyed one small beakful, bites off the head, and then, with a wicked chuckle, proceeds to mete out similar treatment to another head of corn. Needless to say, the villager is no more fond of the parrot than the forest officer is of the villager.

The diet of green parrots is by no means confined to wheat. No grain crop comes amiss to the bird, and, if there be no corn in Egypt, they make merry among the fruit trees. Green parrots are, however, strict vegetarians. I would earnestly commend this fact to those good people who attribute all sin in this world to the eating of meat. Further, green parrots are teetotalers. This should be borne in mind by those who declare that the origin of all crime is to be found in strong drink. Finally, no green parrot is blessed with so much as two coppers to rub against one another. Let those who assert that money is the root of all evil consider this fact. Parrots are vegetarians, teetotalers, and care not for filthy lucre, yet they are steeped in iniquity from birth to death, from egg to exit. But, we may safely leave these momentous facts to moral philosophers and return to the parrot's bump of destructiveness. It is the large development of this appendage which contributes so largely to the bird's enjoyment of life.

That green parrots do derive an exceptionally large amount of enjoyment from existence, no one, who has watched a flock of them, can for a moment doubt. Other causes contribute to this enjoyment of life. One of these is the pleasure—pure and unalloyed pleasure—which these birds derive from annoying other species. A green parrot will gladly take the trouble to deviate from its swift arrow-like course merely to hustle some inoffensive little bird off its perch.

Then again, the tongue of a parrot differs from that of other birds. It is constructed so as to give the bird a strong sense of taste. This is a sense which must be wanting in many birds, else how could they eat worms? Watch a pigeon feeding. This lovable bird will gobble up a couple of hundred grains of Indian corn in half as many seconds, which reminds me of the fact that our Teutonic cousins seem to have queer ideas regarding what constitutes a compliment.

I once heard a German tell an English girl, who was making a very poor dinner, that she had a stomach like a pigeon. It is possible that he meant that her appetite resembled that of a dove. Whatever he meant, he was very pleased with himself, until he saw the expression of anger and disgust on the girl's face. Then he grew sad. Pigeons are very graceful birds, but their manner of eating does not commend itself to our British ideas.

This, however, is a digression. What I want to emphasize is, that a bird which stows away its food at such a rate cannot possibly taste what it is eating. The same applies, in a lesser degree, to a dog. The parrot, however, is an epicure.

Lastly, Polly has an ear for music. Not that its voice is musical. The call of a parrot is a terrible one, and any less optimistic bird would be greatly depressed at having to go through life with a note which, to put it mildly, is an exceedingly harsh squeak. The parrot, however, so far as one can judge, is very proud of its voice. It never loses an opportunity of making itself heard. During its flight it habitually emits loud screeches. Not only is the note harsh and loud, there is in addition something particularly offensive in it. What exactly this is, it is difficult to say, but I feel sure that every one will agree with me when I say that the bird's call is such as to make one want to punch its head!

Evil though their character be, we must admit that green parrots are very beautiful objects. They are ornaments to the scenery of the country. As they fly through the air, they look truly magnificent; Lockwood Kipling has happily called them "live emeralds in the sun."

Parrots are eminently social birds. They almost invariably hunt in little parties of six or seven. They rarely, if ever, alight upon the ground. They delight to sit upon the topmost boughs of trees. At night, they roost together in large flocks, not infrequently in company with crows and mynas.

Green parrots nest in holes. They, as a rule, excavate their own dwellings, their powerful beak being their spade. Green parrots, I think, sometimes utilize a ready-made hole in a tree, if one happens to be available. They certainly often nest in holes in buildings.

I have been assured that these birds sometimes themselves excavate holes in buildings constructed of soft stone. Now, I have very great respect for a parrot's beak; indeed, I positively refuse to handle a strange parrot without first protecting my hands with a pair of driving gloves. Nevertheless, I find it difficult to believe that a green parrot's beak is capable of boring into stone. Even if the feat were possible, I do not think that "poor Polly" would attempt it, for the excavation would certainly give him beak-ache, which must be quite as painful as tooth-ache.

The common green parrot is found all over India, except in the higher hills. Hence those who would escape the noisy cries of our green friends have but to shake the dust of the plains from off their feet and ascend to the abode of the gods. The birds, however, venture up to a height of about five thousand feet in Southern India. Above this they will not trust themselves, for they are tropical birds, and love not a low temperature.

Although green parrots are so widely scattered, they are by no means uniformly distributed through the peninsula. In Bombay, for example, they are almost as numerous as the crows. In Calcutta they are not plentiful, while in Madras one does not see a dozen in the course of the summer. They are more abundant, however, in what those who dwell in the Benighted Presidency speak of as "the cold weather."

This uneven distribution of birds is a curious phenomenon, and many species exhibit it. So far as I know, no satisfactory explanation has been offered. It does not appear to be a question of food-supply or climate, for it often happens that a certain kind of bird is found in only one of two places where the conditions of life appear to be very similar.

There is another common green parrot, the rose-headed paroquet (*P. cyanocephalus*). This is a very beautiful bird, its green body being set off by a red head, having a bloom like that on a plum. It is better mannered than its commoner cousin. It has a more pleasing voice, and affects forests rather than cultivated land. It is, therefore, from the ryot's point of view, a more desirable bird.

Indian parrots are good mimics, and can be taught to talk. The best instructor is a phonograph, which should continually repeat "poor Polly's" lesson. The instrument should be put near the bird's cage and covered up. Then it should be turned on. At first the parrot will be somewhat alarmed. Then its alarm will give place to surprise and curiosity. It will next put its head on one side and listen to the words. After a time, it will try to repeat them. The first attempts will be very feeble ones. A little practice, however, will make Polly perfect. A word of warning is necessary to the would-be instructor of parrots. The phonograph lesson should not last more than twenty minutes, or the poor bird will get brain fever!

In America they have parrot schools, where for a few dollars Polly is given a complete education!

THE TAILOR-BIRD

"A wren, light rustling
Among the leaves and twigs."

WERE a census taken of the birds of Madras, the crows would come easily first on the list; but there would be keen competition between the mynas and the tailor-birds for the second place, and I should hesitate to say whether the sparrows or the king-crows would establish a right to the fourth place, a long way behind the third. Abundant though they be, tailor-birds are unknown to quite a number of people. It is not that they avoid the public gaze or shun the "madding crowd." Far from it. The tailor-bird is essentially a creature of garden and verandah; but he is not arrayed in gay plumage and is very small, so fails to attract the eye. His feathers are of sober hue, but he makes up with vivacity what he lacks in brilliance of plumage.

Little folks tend to be more vivacious than big ones. The reason of this is, I suppose, that the little people have less bulk of body to keep going, and consequently have a larger stock of surplus energy. It is as well that this is so. How ridiculous would a man of 6 feet 5 inches appear who habitually gesticulated and flung himself about like a volatile Frenchman! Equally absurd would a goose be that flirted its tail and hopped about as a tailor-bird does. There are, of course, exceptions to this rule.

Some little men and women are as stolid as buffaloes, and some small birds are as sedate as Mark Twain's frog was after the shot had been administered to it. But these are few and far between. They are merely the exceptions which prove the rule.

I must now describe the tailor-bird, or, to give him his full name and title, *Orthotomus sutorius*. He is just a tiny greenish-brown wren-like bird; indeed, he is a relative of Mistress Jenny Wren, with whom we are so familiar in England.

During the greater part of the year Mr. and Mrs. Durzie are alike in outward appearance. The upper plumage is greenish with a dash of gold or chestnut on the head. This last is set off by a neat black collar, visible only when the neck is stretched; but as the bird cannot sing without stretching its neck, and as it sings, or rather makes a noise, all day long, the black collar is not difficult to distinguish. The lower parts of the bird are dull white, and are thus lighter in colour than the back and wings. This arrangement is very common in nature among many classes of animals.

Of the birds clothed in sombre plumage, such as snipe, sandpipers, and babblers, fully ninety per cent are darker in colour above than below. Paradoxical though it may seem, this distribution of colour causes an animal to be less conspicuous than it would be were it of a uniform brown hue.

This is proved by the following experiment conducted at the Natural History Museum, South Kensington. In a square box, lined with grey flannel, are placed two bird models, which are covered with flannel of the same hue as that which lines the box. One model is painted dark above and white below, the other is left uncoloured, or, rather, is grey all over. The uncoloured bird is the more conspicuous. The painted bird, by counteracting the normal light and shade, becomes at two yards' distance almost invisible. This may be one of the reasons why so many birds, beasts, and fishes are darker in colour above than below.

But to return to the description of the tailor-bird. In the breeding season, that is to say, from April to August, the two middle tail-feathers of the cock bird grow to a greater length than the others and project two inches beyond them as sharp bristles.

Such then are tailor-birds, of which a dozen or more are to be seen in almost every garden in the plains of India, flitting and hopping about among the shrubs and plants looking for insects, and giving vent to their note, which may be syllabized as *to-wit, to-wit, to-wit*, or *pretty, pretty, pretty*. The sound varies greatly with the individual. Some people object to the call of the tailor-bird; they complain that it "gets on their nerves."

Personally, I would not willingly miss the joyous note from the bird-chorus, although I am prepared to say, with Colonel Cunningham, that whilst listening to it "one realizes the beauty of the dispensation that has decreed that in the animal kingdom there should be no necessary direct ratio between size and vocal power; an elephant with a voice on the scale of that of a tailor-bird would have been a nuisance to a whole district."

The tailor-bird is interesting chiefly on account of the nest it constructs, which is one of the most wonderful things in Nature. The nursery in which the young tailors are born is composed of one or more leaves which are sown together by the parents. The bird's beak is its needle, and the cotton is begged, borrowed, or stolen. If the fruit of the silk-cotton tree be ripe, the tailor-bird extracts cotton from this and spins it into thread with beak and feet. If there be no silk-cotton trees in the neighbourhood the bird often has recourse to "the fibrous webbing at the bases of the petioles of the common toddy palm."

A lady who resides in Madras informs me that she once saw a tailor-bird spinning thread for its nest out of a spider's web. The bird of course prefers its cotton thread ready-made when it can find it, so does not hesitate to rifle a lady's work-box if it espies one in an accessible place. I would advise those who are fond of watching birds to leave some pieces of cotton in the verandah during the nesting season, and if there be some cannas among the pot plants the chances are that a pair of tailor-birds will elect to construct a nest in that friendly verandah.

The method of nest-building varies with the kind of

leaf. If it be a large one, the sides are drawn together and stitched to keep them in situ. Exactly how the sewing is performed and the knot made, I do not know. I have not yet had the good fortune to watch the process, nor do I know any person who has. If no large-leafed plants are available in the selected site, the bird has to content itself with smaller leaves, and it sews two or more of these together. A leaf of tough texture is, of course, a *sine quâ non;* one that tears easily would not stand the strain of the weight of a family of young *durzies.* I once came across a nest of which the threads had torn the leaves very badly, and as the youngsters had only just emerged from the eggs, I was afraid they would come to an untimely end; but the leaf did hold out, and the chicks went forth into the world with all their little limbs intact.

The nest, which is thus a kind of purse or pocket, is well lined with cotton or other soft material, and looks remarkably cosy when completed. It is almost invariably placed within three feet of the ground, and is usually in the neighbourhood of a human habitation.

There was a tailor-bird's nest this year in one of the plants outside the verandah of the Grand Stand on the "Island" at Madras. The nests are common enough, but so cunningly are they wrought that they are not easy to find. Last April, a friend of mine was trimming his cannas when he noticed that one of the leaves was withering, so cut it off. After he had severed it from the plant, he discovered in it a nearly completed tailor-bird's nest. He then stuck the leaf back into the pot, hoping that the birds would continue the construction of the nest. But they quickly discovered that something was wrong, held a consultation, and came to the conclusion that the foundations were shaky, so built a second nest on a sound leaf.

As soon as the nursery is ready, three, four, or five diminutive eggs are laid in it. The tailor-bird, like several other species, lays more than one type of egg. In this case there are three varieties: those with a white background with red blotches, those whose surface is white and but faintly speckled with red, and those which have a blue background blotched with red.

This presents a difficult problem to those who believe that birds' eggs are coloured so as to render them inconspicuous. I am unable to share this belief. In nine cases out of ten, eggs are conspicuous objects in a nest, and, even if they were not, it would be difficult to persuade me that a bird, which habitually devours the eggs of other birds, which is, so to speak, a professional egg-stealer, would, when it has once discovered a nest, be deceived into thinking it were empty because its contents were inconspicuously coloured.

When a burglar has broken into a house he does not at once leave it because he does not see the silver on the dining-table. Nor does an egg-stealing bird which has discovered a nest leave it without first carefully scrutinizing the interior. Instinct teaches birds to build their nests in hidden places, and if, in spite of this, the nest is discovered, it is then too late to think of saving the eggs.

The case of those birds which do not construct nests,

but lay their eggs on the bare ground, is very different; such eggs are invariably protectively coloured, and so well do they harmonize with their surroundings that even a trained zoologist may take ten minutes or more to discover a clutch of eggs which he knows to be lying within five yards of where he is standing!

TAILS

THE late Richard Jefferies once defined man as "an animal with arms." The definition, so far as it goes, is a good one, for it is to his arms, quite as much as to his superior brain, that man owes his present supreme position at the head of animal creation.

So much has been written regarding the large brain of man that the other factor which has contributed to his triumph is in danger of being utterly neglected. The arms and brain of man are the two physical necessities to him as a species; take away either, and he becomes something else. To endeavour to decide which of the two organs is the more useful would be as futile as to attempt to prove that the right wheel is more essential to a dog-cart than the left.

Consider what a helpless creature man would be were his arms replaced by a second pair of legs. We human beings would still be dwellers in caves, living in terror of the lion, the tiger, the wolf, and the wild boar. On the other hand, arms, without a suitable brain, will not make a man; for monkeys have arms.

Since the rest of the animals do not possess these organs, they must be very helpless creatures as compared with man. This they indeed are, but not so helpless as might at first be supposed, because they have other compensating organs.

The elephant possesses a trunk which is nearly as useful as an arm. The sensitive upper lip of the horse, the tapir, and other creatures, is a rudimentary prehensile organ—an attempt at a hand. The beak of the parrot, the crow, and the woodpecker, and the claws of most birds perform many of the functions of the human hand. The fore-limbs of some mammals, as, for instance, the bear and the squirrel, are utilized in a similar way.

In addition to these auxiliaries nearly every vertebrate animal boasts a tail. To the naturalist this is perhaps the most interesting of all organs. It is one of the few luxuries which parsimonious Dame Nature allows her children. Always a useful organ, the tail is in hardly a single instance absolutely essential to the existence of its possessor. I doubt if any animal exists that could not manage to jog along through life without its caudal appendage.

The organ seems, so to speak, to have arisen by accident. Without desiring to dogmatise, I think it may be laid down that the early ancestors of the vast majority of existing back-boned animals were amphioxus-like creatures devoid of limbs. When these appendages first budded forth it chanced that the hind pair did not arise at the extreme end of the animal; they took origin some little way forward. And, as the vital organs did not extend to the whole length of the body, there remained a posterior portion of comparative unimportance to its possessor—a quantity of plastic substance capable of being moulded into almost any shape and utilized in all manner of ways.

The fish and the whale needed a propelling organ to enable them the more rapidly to force their way through the water; the tail was pressed into service. The squirrel and the fox felt the want of a warm counterpane to protect them from the chilly blasts of the cold east winds, so Nature took the plastic tail, lengthened it, covered it with thick, soft, fluffy fur, and thus presented the animals with warm quilts.

In other cases Nature has made the tail into a prehensile organ, so that its possessors have become very expert tree-climbers, and are also able to utilize the caudal appendage in carrying their young.

Some creatures inhabit damp marshes and hot countries where flies abound, ready to sting them and worry them to death. A fly-whisk is almost a necessity to such animals, so Nature has made one for them out of their tail.

The skunk hit upon a strange mode of keeping off his enemies. He devised the plan of secreting a fluid emitting the most disgusting odour, so powerful that no animal will willingly venture near him. He needed an advertisement of this fact, lest some animal should attack him in mistake for an inoffensive creature, so his tail was converted into an advertisement board. He trots along slowly with his caudal appendage aloft, and every animal recognizes it, so he is allowed to pass through life unmolested.

The tail is a conspicuous feature in the anatomy of

birds. Most of the fowls of the air are able to boast of a caudal appendage of sorts. Some possess resplendent tails—the products, we are told, of sexual selection, the admiration of the ladies for that which is beautiful. In very many cases the tail acts as a rudder or steering apparatus to its possessor during flight.

This is well seen in the king-crow, the swift, the swallow, and, indeed, in most fly-catching species. The tail feathers of the woodpecker are very stiff and are of great use in helping the bird to maintain its position on the trunks of trees. In nearly every case the tail is of use during the flight of its possessor. Nine birds out of ten spread out their caudal feathers when they take to their wings. The feathers of a bird's tail are arranged so that the tail is almost impervious to air. They are, moreover, provided with powerful muscles, so that when the bird flies they can be spread out in the shape of a fan with a curved surface, the concavity being underneath. This is especially well seen in the flight of a dove or a kite. Nevertheless, the tail is not indispensable to a flying bird.

I once cut off, quite close to their bases, the tail feathers of a pigeon; the bird flew quite easily after the operation. The motion of the wings was perhaps rather more rapid, and the flight generally more laboured; nor did the bird steer itself so well as usual. Therefore, the tail, although both an ornamental and useful organ, is by no means indispensable to a bird. As has before been remarked, the caudal appendage is one of the few luxuries which Nature allows her children.

In the case of some animals, the use of the tail is not

so obvious. Take the lizard as an example. His tail would appear at first sight to be of little or no service to him, since he parts with it so readily. As a matter of fact, the little reptile has many enemies; of these, the Indian crow is the chief. Now, when a crow attacks a lizard, it naturally tries to seize him somewhere near the middle. While the bird is striking at him, the reptile starts to run away; the result is that the crow either misses him or seizes him by the tail. If the latter happens, the tail is swiftly detached, and the lizard makes good his escape.

A few animals possess tails which apparently serve no useful purpose. These are exceedingly interesting creatures, for, if their tails really are useless, they are anomalies that threaten to upset all the theories of biological science. I do not know the use of the tail of the rat, or the mouse. Yet we may be tolerably certain that in each case the organ has some use or it would not exist. I employ the word "use" in a very wide sense. I hold an organ to be useful to an animal if it help its possessors to obtain a mate.

Galton maintains that the action of Natural (or Sexual) Selection is necessary to keep any organ up to the mark; that if the action of Natural Selection is removed from any organ, that organ at once begins to deteriorate. In other words, from the moment an organ becomes useless to its possessor, that organ begins to degenerate, and eventually disappears. Proofs of this are seen throughout the realm of nature.

Many animals which spend their lives in utter darkness, whether in the depths of the ocean, or in caves, have lost not only their sight, but even their eyes. Man's tail became useless to him, so has disappeared. The whale's legs were no longer needed when it took to an aquatic life; they were, therefore, transformed into fins.

Thus it is probable that, if the tails of the mouse and the rat served no useful purpose, these animals would long ago have been reduced to the state of the guinea-pig. What, then, is the use of the tail in each case? This is, indeed, a problem. These creatures, being nocturnal in their habits, do not afford the naturalist many opportunities of watching them. Nevertheless, they move in such a rapid, silent, mysterious way that it is more than possible that the long supple tail assists them during locomotion.

THE KING-CROW

"STURDY independence" sums up the character of the king-crow (*Dicrurus ater*). Needless to state, this royal bird has no connexion with the vulgar, plebeian crow. It is difficult to account for the origin of this popular name. It is true that the king-crow is clothed in glossy, shining black plumage from the top of his head to the tip of his long forked tail, but with this, all resemblance to the *corvi* ceases. The two races have absolutely nothing else in common. They are, moreover, sworn enemies.

Far more appropriate is one of the native names for the bird, the *kotwal;* which, being interpreted, is the head officer of the chief police station. Every one who is acquainted, on the one hand, with the methods of the Indian police, and, on the other, with the habits of the king-crow, will appreciate the title. This bird, who should more properly be called the black drongo, is the chief police officer of the feathered world. He is inspector-general, commissioner, superintendent, inspector and constable, all rolled into one. He takes upon his shoulders the burden of keeping in order the whole bird population of India. His office is no sinecure, for although the fowls of the air are in general law-abiding folk, there are not wanting among them vagabonds, egg-stealers, nest-breakers, and other criminals.

Among birds, as among human beings, the wicked flourish like the green bay tree. Crows, kites, and birds of prey live lives of iniquity, yet they have possessed themselves of the land. They are so numerous that the king-crow is flown off his wings in endeavouring to keep them in something like order. He receives no fixed salary for his police duties.

But, were you to ask the drongo if philanthropic motives prompted him to do this work, he would put his tongue in his cheek and split his sides with laughing. He is an Eastern. He lives up to all the best traditions of the Oriental police by levying blackmail at every opportunity. Moreover, he looks with lenient eye on offences committed against the person or property of others, becoming zealous in his duties only when he has to investigate crimes of which he is the victim.

The king-crow is of opinion that charity begins—and ends—at home. Hence it comes to pass that the police activity of the drongo is greatest during the nesting season. At no other time has the bird any property to look after. Nests are constructed from April to July, and during these months a couple of king-crows chasing a crow or a kite is a sight so common as to attract but little attention.

Nearly every bird, no matter how small or weak, will attack the animal which threatens its nest; in this respect there is nothing remarkable about the king-crow.

He, however, differs from all other birds in the ferocity of his attack and the eagerness with which he rushes into the fray.

Like the London street cad, the king-crow thoroughly enjoys a row. He never loses an opportunity of picking a quarrel. If another bird so much as wink its eye at His Royal Highness, that is held to be sufficient provocation. To venture within twenty yards of the tree in which the royal nest is situated is high treason.

Now, since the drongo's nest is not so large as a lawn-tennis ball, and is usually carefully concealed in a forked branch of a leafy tree, it often happens that a quiet, inoffensive bird, one who has never done anything naughty, innocently settles in the tree only to be roughly handled by the unreasonable owners of the nest. It is superfluous to say that the crow never loses a chance of "taking a rise" out of a king-crow. The interest which the larger bird takes in the nest of the smaller is really quite affecting.

A crow is pottering about aimlessly, looking out for mischief for idle claws to do, when it observes a couple of drongos busily at work. "A nest, probably young ones!" says Mr. Corvus Splendens to his noble self. He then proceeds to wend his way towards the king-crows, sailing along with that air of jaunty nonchalance which cats and crows alone can assume.

"Morning! How's the nest and the dear little angels?" caws he. In less time than it takes to relate, the irate drongos have dashed at the crow, and are trying to secure beakfuls of feathers out of his back.

The last-named is beating a hasty and somewhat undignified retreat; he is half sorry he came, his joy at having angered the king-crows being tempered by the fear of parting with a portion of his plumage.

The king-crow is the pluckiest of birds. It is difficult to name the creature of which he is afraid. One day I happened to pass under a low tree in which some drongos were sitting. These birds began to swear lustily. I looked up to investigate the phenomenon, and saw that there were in the tree three young king-crows, fresh from the nest and scarcely able to fly.

The birds were out of my reach, but notwithstanding this the parents fluttered about my head in a state of great excitement. Had I touched one of the youngsters the father and mother would probably have attacked my hand, and tried to take pieces of flesh out of it.

I once saw a couple of drongos treat a monkey very shamefully. The mammal was squatting in the middle of the road, and, to avoid the wheels of my cart and the lash of my whip, took refuge in a *neem* tree.

Now this tree happened to contain a king-crow's nest. Before the monkey was half-way up the tree the drongos were taking pecks at his head. The ape looked very hurt at this outbreak of Hooliganism, having of course no idea that the birds were merely protecting their nest. He jumped into the next tree, but the attack continued with unabated fury.

So the monkey moved on again, but the king-crows still continued to make dashes at his head, which must have been aching badly by this time. The monkey then jumped on to the ground and cowered at the base of the trunk of a tree.

Still the little furies made swoops at him, so that he took to his heels and ran until he had put a long distance between himself and his foes.

I think sufficient has been said to show that king-crows are able to look after their nests.

Before passing on to consider some other traits of their sturdy character, a few words about the nest and eggs may not be out of place. The former is "a strong, neat cup of roots and grass," covered over with cobwebs. It looks rather like a knot in a tree and hence is very difficult to distinguish when the bird is not sitting. The eggs are remarkable as being of three distinct types. They may be pure white, the ground colour may be white, spotted with red, or the general colour may be salmon, spotted with red, brown, and purple.

This is, I think, a very hard nut for those to crack who maintain that eggs laid in nests are protectively coloured. Needless to say, the same kind of young bird comes out of each description of egg. The young, when they first leave the nest, closely resemble their parents, the chief point of difference being that the lower plumage is spotted with white or grey. The adult king-crow is a most beautiful object. Its beauty is that of form and proportion rather than of colour. It is the beauty of the athlete, of the racehorse, of the tiger.

King-crows need to be of athletic build, for they live exclusively on flies and insects, which they catch on the wing. Their method of securing a meal is simple. It is to take up a position on the back of a cow, or horse (far enough forward to avoid the swish of the tail), on a bare branch, a railing, a telegraph pole, or any other "rod, pole or perch" from which a good outlook can be obtained. From this point of vantage they make little sallies into the air after insects. It is at this juncture that the king-crow's forked tail is useful; it is by no means a mere ornament; it is the bird's rudder, and a most efficient steering apparatus it makes. The aerial movements of a king-crow, its graceful flight, its rapid turns, its elegant curves, compel admiration. The chased insect has not the ghost of a chance.

Not long ago I witnessed a most interesting insect-catching match at the Gymkhana Club, Madras, between the crows and the drongos. It was a case of Gentlemen *v.* Players. The crows were the Gentlemen. I use the word in its strict sporting sense. As to social status, the crow is on a par with the professional card-sharper, but as regards fly-catching he is an amateur.

It was Sunday evening, when, the Gymkhana being deserted by human beings, the birds were able to enjoy themselves without let or hindrance. The king-crows were perched on the white railings, while the crows were on the ground inside the enclosure. The sun had just disappeared below the horizon and insects innumerable were upon the wing. These were the quarry. The king-crows won the toss and put the crows in first. As an insect came conveniently near, a crow made a dash at it and in most cases missed it, then a king-crow would capture it and thereby score a point. The "Pros" literally "ran round" the amateurs.

Never before has a more crushing defeat been inflicted upon an amateur team. Time after time the drongos succeeded where the crows had failed. It was amusing to compare the clumsy attempts of the *corvi* with the neat, clean curves and turns of the drongos. But the crows, although outclassed, did not give in. The contest lasted until the umpires decided that the light was too bad for play, and so ordered stumps to be drawn.

Another proof of the masterful character of the king-crow is the small amount of sleep in which he indulges. Great men and drongos allow themselves only about five hours' sleep in the twenty-four. The king-crows are always the last of the birds to go to bed and are usually the earliest to rise. Long before dawn, the cheery, metallic, whistling note of the king-crow is to be heard.

A short time ago one of these birds tuned up at 2.30 a.m. In the middle of the day they do not sing much; they are too earnestly engaged in the business of life to indulge in the "chanting of foolish litanies" and the like frivolities, but, as the sun begins to approach the horizon, they allow themselves a little relaxation in form of song.

In spite of all his cleverness, the king-crow is victimized by a cuckoo. But we may say this for him, that he is the dupe of no clumsy hoax. The cuckoo in question is able to gain access to the nest only by donning the plumage of the king-crow. The disguise is almost perfect, the only flaw being that the cuckoo is not able to disguise its zygodactyle feet. But the king-crow does not notice such trifles. If he did he would probably take the wily cuckoo for a deformed cousin and offer him a ticket for a free dinner at the nearest charitable institute.

CONCERNING CATS

HISTORY does not record the name of the person who first conceived the idea of domesticating the cat. All we know with certainty is that the individual in question was not an Englishman. Some people, learned in philology, assert that pussy was first domesticated in Persia. The evidence upon which this theory is based is the name "Puss," which is alleged to be a corruption of "Perse." Personally, I would not hang a dog, much less consign a cat to Persia, upon such evidence.

Wherever it was first domesticated, the cat soon came to occupy a high position in human esteem. This is proved by the fact that cat mummies have been discovered in Egypt, where temples were dedicated to the quadruped. How the creature succeeded in thus ingratiating itself is a mystery to me. I have studied the ways of the animal for some years, and have been unable to discover a shred of respectability about pussy's character. It is true that I admire the magnificent way in which the cat always falls on its feet when thrown out of the window. I once saw a cat flung from the third floor of a London house. Puss fell lightly on her feet and strolled off in a most dignified manner.

The cat is an ungrateful creature; she attaches herself to localities, not to persons. Cat-lovers will probably take exception to this assertion; but let them for a moment compare their cats with their dogs. How many cats have they possessed that would follow them about wherever they went and refuse to leave them unless tied up, or held back by force? How many cats have they owned that would receive them with great demonstrations of joy after a short absence? How many cats have they known that would invariably come to their owner when called? These are all attributes of even a poor pariah dog.

The cat is selfishness personified. It is a discontented creature, and manifests its discontent by emitting that most abominable of sounds—a miau. It is sly, cunning, and not over-valorous. It dislikes a bath, and is, as a rule, incapable of real affection. It is a savage, which has lost few of its ancestral traits. It is the most contemptible member of the most cruel family of mammals.

"No creature," writes Lockwood Kipling, "is more independent than the cat. Its more complete domestication in the West is in reality mainly due to its love of warmth. For the sake of comfort it will tolerate humanity, and blink amiably at the fireside, but a serene selfishness is at the basis of its character. The Indian domestic cat is not bound to the family circle by the need of warmth; there is no fireside to speak of, and it lives its own life."

Pussy consents to be semi-domesticated in the West because she is cute enough to know that she is a gainer thereby. She is petted and pampered, so in return "blinks amiably" at, and purrs to, her benefactor. There is no denying the fact that the cat is a very intelligent animal. Feline toleration of the human race is, then, comprehensible; but why do so many human beings love the cat?

One can of course easily understand why the whole race of domestic servants in Europe look with kindly eyes upon the miniature tiger. It is the scapegoat of the genus servitor. It bears the burden of many breakages of crockery, not all of course; to ascribe to pussy *all* the damage sustained by the household china would be tantamount to killing the goose that lays the golden eggs, for it would lead inevitably to the rapid expulsion of the cat—hence it happens that articles of crockery have a foolish and disagreeable habit of coming to pieces in the hands. Oh! fragile cups and saucers, why come asunder at the gentle touch of Mary Ann?

Then, again, cats keep down the population of mice, hence the affection with which servants regard poor pussy. But this does not explain the love which the elderly spinster of all classes entertains towards a most objectionable quadruped. Victor Hugo has, I think, discovered the reason. According to him, "*Dieu a fait le chat pour donner á l'homme le plaisir de caresser le tigre.*"

People keep cats just because cats are *felidæ*. The cat is obviously a tiger in miniature, hence the fascination which it exercises over the human mind.

In the Middle Ages cats were feared rather than loved, and, as we shall see, cats are not now, nor ever have been, universally popular. The mysterious air of the cat, its nocturnal habits, its terrible caterwaulings, which often sound like the cries of human beings in distress, and its shining orbs, all tended to cause the belief that cats were witches' familiars.

Sailors, who are invariably superstitious, object to having cats on a ship; but when once a cat finds its way on board it is usually allowed to remain there, for, were pussy thrown overboard, a furious storm would assuredly arise.

Before passing on to demonstrate the popular dislike of cats, let me quote the excellent description of the animal given by Bartholomew Angelicus: "He is a full lecherous beast in youth, swift, pliant, and merry, and leapeth and reseth on everything that is afore him, and is led by a straw and playeth therewith, and is a right heavy beast in age and full sleepy, and lieth slyly in wait for mice, and is aware where they be more by smell than by sight, and hunteth and reseth on them in privy places, and when he taketh a mouse he playeth therewith, and eateth him after the play. In time of love is hard fighting for wives, and one scratcheth and rendeth the other grievously with biting and with claws, and he maketh a rueful noise and ghastful when one preferreth to fight with another, and hardly is he hurt when he is thrown down off an high place. And when he hath a fair skin he is, as it were, proud thereof, and goeth fast about, and is oft for his fair skin taken of the skinner and slain and flayed."

As evidence of the general and, as I think, well-founded dislike of the cat, I may cite the distich which often accompanies the signpost on inns, bearing the sign of "The Cat and Lion":—

> "The lion is strong, the cat is vicious,
> My ale is strong, and so is my liquors."

A Frenchman named Bertrand had to leave his native country in a hurry, having been detected in a plot against Cardinal Mazarin. He fled to the Hague, where he opened a cutler's shop, setting up as a sign a picture representing a cat and the Cardinal and wrote under it: "*Aux deux méchantes bêtes.*"

Among the natives of India, too, the cat does not seem to be popular. This is evidenced by many native proverbs. I quote two from Lockwood Kipling: "The cat with mouse tails still hanging out of her mouth says: 'Now I feel good, I will go on a pilgrimage to Mecca,'" and "The cat does not catch mice for God." Some people not merely dislike cats, they loathe them with a great loathing. Napoleon was a case in point.

Henry III of France is said to have fainted at the mere sight of a cat. But the gentleman who "takes the cake" is he who wrote many years ago to the "Spectator": "As I was going through a street of London, where I had never been till then, I felt a general clamp and faintness all over me, which I could not tell how to account for, till I chanced to cast my eyes upwards, and found that I was passing under a signboard on which the picture of a *cat* was hung!"

Even nowadays many people declare that they cannot bear to be in the same room as a cat, a black one for preference; they assert that they can feel an uncanny presence, even though the quadruped be not visible.

Personally, I have no objection to the company of a well-behaved cat, but "poor puss" is not an animal which appeals to me. I have lived too long in London to cherish any friendly feelings towards the feline race. Too often have I been awakened by the caterwaulings which nightly emanated from some roof of bad repute.

We were unfortunate enough to have as our next-door neighbour a lady novelist. "The woman writer," says Mr. Crosland, "is an offence in the sight of Olympus." This sentiment seems scarcely polite, and I am not prepared to subscribe to it until I have discovered whether every feminine author keeps a Cats' Home, as the lady writer in question did. The good woman loved cats.

Now, to all those who are similarly disposed towards pussy I would respectfully say: "Remember that cats are not what they seem. During the day they look as though butter would not melt in their mouths; they appear to be paragons of virtue, models of saintliness. But what a difference in the night! Then they become fiends incarnate.

"Remember, ye possessors of cats, that you get the benefit of your pets by day, but your neighbours get it by night. You cannot keep cats and be popular." To the neighbours I would say: "Keep an air gun." I speak as one having special knowledge. I lived for years next door to the aforesaid Cats' Home, and succeeded in keeping the inmates on their side of the garden wall. A cat, when once it has received the charge from a "Gem" air gun, is a remarkably wary animal. No cat ever ventured outside that Home without keeping an eye on the windows of our house. If any one appeared at a window the cat would show a turn of speed that would do credit to any greyhound.

I remember on one occasion looking out of the window and seeing the lady novelist stroking "dear pussy." The creature was purring contentedly, and all went well until it happened to catch sight of me. In less time than it takes to say "Jack Robinson" that cat had put three gardens between itself and me. The astonishment of the lady writer at the seemingly extraordinary behaviour of "puss" was good to watch. But cats are not without their redeeming features. They catch mice, and the bolder spirits among them will stand up to a rat.

Further, the veneer of domestication covers the cat so scantily that it is scarcely necessary to go into the wilderness in order to study the ways of the *felidæ* in a state of nature. It suffices to watch puss. Note the stealth with which she walks and the noiselessness of her footfall. Contrast her silent gait with the noisy pitter-patter of the dog. There is, of course, no necessity for pussy to walk as though she were dodging a policeman; this practice is the survival of a trait useful, nay indispensable, to the wild species, which have to stalk over dried grass and shrivelled leaves a prey which is keen of hearing and fleet of foot. Notice the tremendous speed at which a cat can run and the mighty springs of which she is capable. The best manner of witnessing this is to throw a jug of cold water over the cat when she is asleep in the garden.

Observe how cunning pussy is when engaged in *shikar.* Notice the crouching attitude she adopts and the stealthy manner in which she advances towards her victim. Mark the tail: the tip is raised and is slowly wagged from side to side. This is the only sign given by the cat of the intense excitement with which she is thrilled. A sportsman in India may, if he be fortunate, see a tiger do all this.

The nocturnal proclivities of puss are nothing but a survival of the habits of her ancestors. Most, if not all, her cousins in the wild state hunt during the hours of darkness. Their eyes are made for night-work.

There is, however, one difference between the cat and wild carnivora which it is important to notice, otherwise he who watches pussy will entertain an exaggerated idea of the cruelty of beasts of prey. When a cat catches a mouse she tortures her victim before she actually kills it. I do not think that the mouse suffers much pain while the cat is indulging in her cruel play at its expense. The little rodent is, I believe, half-paralysed, and its senses completely numbed.

Men who have been carried off by lions declare that they experienced no fright; that, indeed, they scarcely realized what was happening. Be this as it may, pussy entreats her victim thus shamefully because she is not hungry; she indulges in *shikar* for pleasure, and not to satisfy a craving for food.

The wild carnivora, although they thoroughly enjoy

hunting, rarely attack other creatures unless driven to do so by the pangs of hunger. Under such circumstances, a beast of prey does not "play" with its victim; it gives it the happy despatch immediately on catching it and proceeds to devour it. The tragedies of nature are usually accompanied by but little cruelty.

A LITTLE NURSERY AND ITS OCCUPANTS

A PAIR of white-browed fantail flycatchers (*Rhipidura albifrontata*) were considerate enough to build a nest within a hundred yards of the house in which I spent a month's leave at Coonoor. The nest in question was placed on a forked branch, the lowest in the tree, and at a height of about ten feet from the ground. I use the past tense advisedly, for the nest is no longer in the tree.

After it had been vacated by the birds I had it removed, and it is now the property of the Bombay Natural History Society. The tree in which the nest was built grows on the slope of a steep hill, so that one had only to ascend a couple of paces in order to look right down into the nest. This latter is a work of art.

If you would make an imitation of it, and, no matter how deft your fingers be, the imitation would, I fear, fall far short of the genuine article, you had best purchase a small bunch of violets. The bunch should be of the description sold by flower-girls for button-holes. It should be well put together, the stalks being tightly bound up with any fibrous material.

Having secured the bunch, the next thing to do is to cut away the heads of the flowers, together with the upper parts of the stems, until you have a hollow cup, of which the base is formed of stalks closely pressed together, and the sides of leaves. This must now be lined with soft material of which the strands should be delicately interwoven, and then, if a few cobwebs be wound outside the stalks, you will have a tolerable imitation of a fantail flycatcher's nest.

The Madras Museum possesses a specimen, but this is not nearly so well put together as the one I am describing. Birds of the same species display different degrees of skill in the construction of their nests. Some are more artistic than others. The fantail flycatcher's nest seems absurdly small for the bird. This has to sit *on* the nest, not *in* it.

Imagine a canary resting on an egg-cup, and you will have some idea of the picture presented by the sitting fantail. In this elegantly-shaped, shallow, cup-like nursery are deposited three cream-coloured eggs, spotted with greyish brown. They are conspicuous objects and may be distinguished at a distance of ten or twelve feet.

This is one of the many awkward facts which confront, at every turn, those naturalists who maintain that all birds' eggs are coloured so as to render them inconspicuous when in the nest. It seems to me that such men are slaves of a theory. So imbued are they with the doctrine of protective colouration that they are unable to see things as they are. But this is a digression.

The eggs require ten or twelve days for their incubation. I believe that both birds sit alternately. When the young hatch out they are of course ugly, large-mouthed creatures, innocent of a single feather. At first, they are very weak, and seem to have scarcely strength enough to raise their heads to receive the insects brought by their parents.

Their growth is, however, exceedingly rapid. When three days old they are fully twice the size they were when first hatched. They keep their fond parents very busy seeking food for them. This consists entirely of minute insects. Many of these are picked off the trunks and branches of trees, some are taken off the ground, while others are caught on the wing. Elegance marks every movement of the fantail flycatcher. It runs swiftly among the branches, and every now and again makes a pretty bow and spreads its tail; then suddenly it will make a little sally in the air, and return, with easy sweep, to the place whence it started. In grace of movement a fantail flycatcher is nearly equal to a wagtail.

While seeking for food the parents never go far from the nest. They keep a most jealous guard over this precious structure, and most necessary is it that they should do so, for crows are exceedingly fond of eating young birds, and are always on the look out for a nest; and when they discover it, woe betide the occupants! "Eha" thus describes this phase of the corvine character, and that which he says is but too true: "What I cannot forgive is the constant and ruthless massacre of innocents that goes on where crows are allowed to have their own way. They watch every little bird to find out if it has a nest; they count the days till the first young sparrow flutters out on its untried wings; they pounce upon it and carry it to the nearest tree and hold it under one foot and pick it to pieces, absolutely callous to the shrieks of the parents as they flutter round, distracted but helpless.

Small wonder, then, that every tiny bird hates the crow with all the hatred of which its little heart is capable. The crows caused these flycatchers much annoyance. I was watching them performing their nursery duties on the second day after their chicks were hatched, when a great black corby alighted in the next tree. Both fantail flycatchers immediately attacked it, screaming angrily.

Their method of procedure was to make a series of dashes at the back and tail of the crow, pecking at it each time they approached. The crow did not appear to mind this treatment very much. It took it very philosophically. It, however, kept a keen eye on its puny aggressors, and, now and again, tried to seize one with its great beak, but they were always too quick for it. The crow was looking about intently, doubtless trying to locate the nest, for the conduct of the fantails betrayed the fact that it was not far off. In spite of the united efforts of the flycatchers, the crow maintained its position. Presently it began to caw. This brought up another "treble-dated bird." The flycatchers then directed their attack against the new-comer, leaving the first crow alone for a little.

Both corbies now began to caw loudly. After the gallant little flycatchers had made over fifty dashes at

THE INDIAN CORBY

it, the second crow flew to a distance of a few yards. The flycatchers again transferred their attention to the first crow, which had maintained its position and was still, I believe, looking about for the nest. Presently the combined attack grew too hot for it, and it flew away. Then the flycatchers re-transferred their attention to the second crow, which eventually moved on. So excited had the fantails become that they continued to scream and swear for some time after the corbies had departed.

But, after a little, they calmed down and resumed their search for food. The crows annoyed them in this way not once, but many times. A few days later I saw these birds mob another crow. The attack lasted fully five minutes. This time it was well arranged. The flycatchers took up positions on each side of the crow and made alternate dashes at it. The corby had its work cut out in defending itself. I never before saw a crow display so much agility. Eventually it grew tired of twisting its head from side to side and flew off.

Being much interested in the plucky manner in which the little birds drove off the crows, I thought I would see what they would do to me if I made as if to take their young ones. Accordingly, when both the parents were near by, I moved up to the nest and stretched out my hand towards it, but it was just out of reach.

The flycatchers made no attempt to attack me. I think they were afraid of so large a creature as a human being. When such birds as bulbuls, babblers, and white-eyes alighted in the tree, in which the nest was situated, the flycatchers did not molest them. Their instinct taught them that these mild birds would not harm their young. But all crows, kites, and hawks that ventured near were promptly mobbed.

By the third day, the young birds had grown so big that there was no room for them to lie side by side in the nest. They lay jumbled together in a heap, of which the summit was higher than the walls of the nursery. By this time the tail and great wing-feathers had begun to appear; these, being in sheaths, made their possessors look like miniature porcupines.

Their conduct in the nest was unlike that of any other young birds I have seen. As a rule, the moment a parent arrives, up into the air go all the gaping mouths, and there is quite a hullabaloo, each youngster being afraid he will be forgotten!

When the parent fantail came to the nest there was no clamour among the young birds, and only one of the three mouths opened. The decorous conduct of the young flycatchers is, probably, to be attributed to the action of natural selection; for, living as they do in such an insecure nursery, the young birds would almost certainly fall out if they were of restless disposition, or if, when the parents came to the nest, they clamoured violently for food.

From the third to the sixth day the young birds did not make any great visible progress. But from the sixth day onwards they developed apace. On the eighth day the white feathers on the eyebrow began to show themselves, and on the tenth the young birds looked quite presentable. The body was then covered with downy feathers, those of the wings and tail being fully developed and the white eyebrow completely formed.

I had to leave Coonoor on the eleventh day after the young birds were hatched, so was unable to witness the first lesson in flying, which was given when they were fourteen days old.

What human play or pageant is so entertaining as the sight of young birds making their first attempts at flight? The excited parents, while giving vent to twitters of endearment and encouragement, make little sallies into the air by way of example. They are saying, in bird language, "Come, my dears, you are quite old enough to fly. See how easy it is and how delightful." But the young birds seem disinclined to emulate their parents. They look fearfully around them.

Again and again, the old birds exhort them; but the young ones still hesitate. They are afraid to trust themselves to their feeble little wings, just as a child, who cannot swim, fears to plunge, head first, into the still water of a swimming-bath.

Eventually the bravest of the little creatures overcomes its fears, and, amid the delighted cries of its parents, essays a short flight. It flutters awkwardly, but manages to reach a neighbouring branch, upon which it alights, trembling with excitement and exultation. The battle is now half won. The other nestlings follow the good example, and, one by one, they learn how delicious is the sensation of sailing on outstretched wings through the thin air.

THE SURVIVAL OF THE UNFIT

IN the Garden of India there is a little hillock of which I wot—a mound raised by the hand of man from the great level plain. Upon the summit stands the ruin of a Muhammadan tomb. The white veneer of marble has fallen away, leaving bare the cold greystone of the domed roof and the crumbling bricks of the massive walls. The white gown with which man clothed the building has been swept away by Nature to be replaced by a garment woven in her own loom—a garment composed of flowered weeds and soft green moss. Apart from its ruined state, the solidity of the pile proves that it belongeth not to this superficial age.

Beneath the dome lie the ashes of some great warrior, long since dead, whose very name seems to have passed from the memory of man. His bones lie neglected, for his whole race has died out.

From the mound a panorama of the fertile plain is obtained. Exuberant life is visible all around. A pied kingfisher (*ceryle varia*) hovers over the lake near by; little birds are singing in the greenwood tree; flocks of boisterous "green parrots" (*Palæornis torquatus*) hurry overhead, nor do they hush their shrill voices as they fly past the abode of the dead. Hard by, from behind a picturesque bamboo clump, ascends the blue smoke from a tiny hamlet.

Some of the little naked village children are actually playing among the ruins of the tomb. It is an interesting sight this. Those children are the sons of the soil, they are little plebeians, descendants of the men who once cringed and cowered before him whose tomb is now a ruin, whose race is extinct, and whose very name has been forgotten. How are the mighty fallen!

Is not this a case of the survival of the unfit? Is it not a paradox that the race of puny, ill-fed men should have survived, while that of the warrior chieftain, superior in intellect and physique, should have become extinct?

But look! two jackals are making their way out of the cover at the base of the mound. Timid creatures these, they look the picture of cowardice as they sneak along, the tail between the legs. Is this not another instance of the survival of the unfit? How is it that these poor fear-stricken jackals are a flourishing species, found all over India, while mighty animals, such as the elephant, the lion, the giraffe, and the tiger, are fast disappearing from off the face of the earth? The question may be extended. How comes it that rats, mice, moles, rabbits, hares, and the other small fry of the mammalian world hold their own in the struggle for existence, while the mammoth, the mastodon, the glyptodon, the giant sloth and the great pterodactyle reptiles have become extinct? What mean these para-

PIED KINGFISHER

doxes? How reconcile them with the doctrine of the survival of the fittest?

In Nature the battle is not always to the strong, nor the race to the swift. The survival of the fittest does not mean the survival of the ideally fit, but of those best adapted to their surroundings. Many are the habitations of the earth, and Nature fills each of these with the most suitable occupant at her disposal. Every creature that now exists is a victor in the struggle for existence. Every one has been offered a situation by Nature and accepted it. The mole survives, not because he is a magnificent, comely creature, but because he is willing to live a lowly life under the earth. The brown rat flourishes because it is ready, for the sake of life, to live in dark, noisome drains and eat garbage.

Every animal now living has survived, because it is willing to occupy the place assigned to it by Nature, no matter how lowly that position be. Many animals have, to use a figure of speech, preferred to perish to thus occupying menial positions; they have refused to accept the station offered them by Nature; they have elected to wage war with the giants of the earth and have been defeated, and hence are known to us only as fossils.

Other great animals have, so to speak, overreached themselves, and hence are no more. There is no room on this little earth for giants. They have all become extinct, with the exception of the elephant, the whale, and the giraffe, and these species are struggling against their inevitable doom. So that even before man came upon the scene, those animals to survive were by no means always the ideally fit, but those who were best able to adapt themselves to the nook or cranny in the world that Nature assigned to them. Man, however, has been more ruthless than even Nature in the destruction of the nobler mammals.

There is an ancient fable that tells of a staunch old oak and a feeble sapling which grew side by side in a forest. A mighty tempest came, the oak tree bravely held up its head and haughtily refused to bow down before the storm, so it was uprooted and died a noble death. The sapling, on the other hand, meekly bent before the stormy blast, acknowledging its supremacy; so the gale passed over it leaving it unharmed.

This fable explains the survival of the unfit.

Before man was evolved the world may be compared to India in pre-British times. There were conquering species and conquered ones. No one race stood head and shoulders above all the rest. Now one species established a supremacy, now another, but the position was invariably a short-lived one, and, even while it lasted, was constantly in jeopardy.

In those days, great pachyderms disputed with monster edentates and powerful carnivora the supremacy of the earth; sometimes one prevailed for a little, sometimes another. Often these conquering species existed side by side, maintaining a kind of armed neutrality, half afraid of each other, and contemptuous of the great mass of the animals, allowing them to occupy those places in the earth which they themselves could not fill. Then suddenly one species prevailed.

This mammal was of no great size, nor was it very muscular. Physically it was by no means the finest of the denizens of the earth. It, however, turned into a weapon an organ which hitherto had not been held of much account—the brain. By using this wonderful organ it learned to defeat strength by craft; it further learned that it was possible to adapt its environment to itself, instead of adapting itself to the environment, as all other animals were compelled to do.

But, for a long while the contest hung in the balance. In spite of his large brain, in spite of the fact that he was able to make implements of stone with which he could sometimes kill the great carnivora, these latter would often seize and devour man, so that he was forced to take shelter in caves. But, as time wore on, his brain enlarged; he grew more skilful in the manufacture of weapons, and soon asserted his supremacy. He has not spared his mighty adversaries. One by one he has swept them off the face of the earth, or forced them to take refuge far from him in swampy places and impenetrable jungles.

The big herbivorous animals he had to destroy, for they required too much food. The elephant and the camel he has allowed to remain because they have consented to act as his slaves. But every great and powerful animal, which refused to recognize his ascendancy, has been swept off the face of the earth, or is being hunted to extinction, so that our present fauna is but a pigmy remnant. All that which is noblest has disappeared.

Were I a poet I would write an ode to the gigantic

animals which have found this little earth too small for them; to the mighty flying reptiles the expanse of whose leathery wings measured thirty feet, and which, had they lived in these days, would have been capable of flying off with a bullock; to the great sloth-like creatures—megatherium, glyptodon, and mylodon—whose height was three times that of a tall man and twice that of the average elephant; to the huge hairy mammoths; to the giant mastodons, whose tusks were twelve feet in length; to the enormous lizards which were large enough to swallow a sheep at a gulp; to the moa, once "the lord of the great Polynesian islands of New Zealand."

When we contemplate such extinct monsters which must be numbered among the unfit, the words "survival of the fittest" acquire a new significance.

COCK ROBIN'S MURDERER

NO bird, except possibly the Indian crow, has been the object of so much vilification as the sparrow:

> "The spink and the sparrow
> Are the devil's bow and arrow."

So runs the country adage, and the farmers act up to its sentiments. They unite to form "sparrow clubs." These benevolent institutions are founded with the pious object of destroying as many as possible of the arrows of the Prince of Darkness. But the hatred of the sparrow is by no means confined to the yokel.

Respectable ornithologists vie with one another in inventing hard names for the pushing little bird. Thus Lord Lilford called him *Passer inpudicus;* Tristram dubs him *Passer papisticus.* Even more scathing is Irby's name for him—*Passer damnabilis.* These denominations, however, all pale into insignificance before the expressive epithet of the farm labourer, which may be Latinized into *Passer sanguineus!*

"The sparrow," writes Masius, "is a vulgar bird—a proletarian, with all the cunning and vices of his class. Slight and persecution are his inheritance. Even in the Bible it is said, 'Are not two sparrows sold for a farthing?' and in Aristophanes even seven are offered for an obole. His dirty colour, his brown jacket, his reddish-brown head and sooty cheeks, his dumpy figure, his bustly flight, gait, voice, demeanour—in short, all betray his low birth and vulgar mind.

"But the Pariah avenges himself on the society which has expelled him by his truly cynical shamelessness. . . . The sparrow is an Atheos, a wild Communist, but shrewd, active, and untiring. . . . When the bold vagabond has fixed himself anywhere neither force nor cunning is able to turn him out. Not in vain has he associated with men, and learned from them craft and wickedness. It is not easy to scare this paragon of audacity, or to inspire him with respect. He is more than a sceptic; he is a decided freethinker. In presumptuous security, he seats himself on the nose or arm of the fluttering, clappering ghost, to whom the charge of the garden is committed. In its very shadow he bids it defiance, and thus, it may be said, enjoys the fruit of his wickedness with a heightened consciousness of his transgression. If he has happily escaped from a net or a pea-shooter, he makes a tremendous outcry; jeers at and abuses the awkward fowler from his hiding-place, and anon the whole scoundrelly fraternity chime in with all the power of their lungs."

This was, of course, written of the sparrow as he is found in Europe. The Indian bird, although he belongs to the same species—*Passer domesticus*—can give his Western cousin points in the matter of evil-doing. "London sparrows," writes Lockwood Kipling, "are said to be familiar, but when compared with their

Indian brethren their manners are marked by dignity and cold reserve." This savours of exaggeration. Under no circumstances whatever can any sparrow be dignified. Add 25 per cent to the impudence, 20 per cent to the rowdyness, and 15 per cent to the vulgarity of the cockney bird, and you will arrive at a tolerably accurate estimate of the character of the sparrow that torments us who live in this Land of Regrets.

Far be it from me to attempt to whitewash the sparrow. I merely desire to present him in his true colours. This being so, I cannot help saying that the bird is not so black as he is depicted. He possesses the virtues of his class equally with its vices. Like the London cad, the sparrow is ever ready for a fight. He allows himself to be drawn into an affray on the smallest pretext. He is not wanting in pluck, for he does not hesitate to attack a bird several sizes larger than himself. This, however, is somewhat discounted by the fact that he is perfectly well aware that, the moment the fight begins, all his companions will come to his assistance.

Still, the sparrow is a bold bird. His supreme indifference to the crows is a sufficient proof of this. Nor is he afraid of man. I once stayed in an hotel in India in which a colony of sparrows had taken up their quarters, and enjoyed board and residence free of charge. At meal times ten or twenty of them would take up positions on the ledge of a dormer window and thence swoop down upon the edibles whenever an opportunity presented itself. The sparrow is said to be terribly destructive to crops. So he is, but this is because he is so numerous. We should also bear in mind that he destroys large quantities of insects, some of which are presumably injurious ones. Sparrows, in moderation, probably conduce to the welfare of the farmer; but, unfortunately, it is not often that we have sparrows in moderation. The truth of the matter is that it is not so much what he does as the way in which he does it that makes the sparrow so offensive.

For example, any fair-minded person will allow that when a cock bird goes a-courting that bird is at liberty to make a fool of itself. The sparrow, of course, does this, and, if he ended here, no one would have a word to say against the proceeding. But unfortunately the sparrow is not satisfied merely with acting idiotically. He insists on selecting for his trysting-place the window-ledge of a busy man's study, and drives the unfortunate occupant to the verge of madness by his "swellings" and his "turkey-cocks." Nor is this the worst feature in the sparrow's courtship. If the amatory professions of the bird were genuine, if all his bowing and scraping were the true outward expression of his inward feelings, one would be content to put up with a great deal at his hands.

As a matter of fact, sparrows of either sex are incapable of any real conjugal affection. Cowper discovered this trait in passerine character and thus expressed himself:—

> "The sparrow, meanest of the feathered race,
> His fit companions finds in every place,
> With whom he filches the grain that suits him best,
> Flits here and there, and late returns to rest;

> And whom if chance the falcon makes his prey,
> Or hedger with his well-aimed arrow slay,
> In no such loss the gay survivor grieves,
> New love he seeks, and new delight receives."

The above is gospel truth.

I know a man who once slew in succession seven cock-sparrows. It happened in this wise. A couple of sparrows determined to build in his verandah. He willed otherwise, and, by way of showing that he meant what he said, murdered the cock-bird. Did the widowed hen sit and mope? Did she shed tears of lamentation? Did she call upon the gods to witness the cruel blow that had fallen upon her? Did she "in soft murmurs tell the trees her pain"? Nothing of the kind. For a minute or so she swore lustily at the slayer of her husband; she then flew away, to return five minutes later with a second husband, and together they set to work at the nest.

The second cock-bird shared the fate of number one. The hen-sparrow then returned with number three, and continued to replace her murdered husbands until she had lured six to their destruction. Then my friend stayed his hand. He was prostrated by the cruel and cynical heartlessness of the hen-sparrow. But she had her own way. She brought up a family in that verandah.

I do not hold it to be an offence for a bird to build its nest inside my house, provided the bird does not molest the human inhabitants of the building. If a winged creature chooses to rear a family in the space between the ceiling-cloth and the rafters of my bungalow, I say, by all means let it do so. That is not the site I should have selected for a habitation, were I a bird, but that is neither here nor there; if the dirty, dark hole meets with the approval of the sparrow, let it bring up its family in it. It is only when the parents insult me every time they enter or leave the nest, that I begin to grow angry with the birds.

I naturally ask what I have done that they should wake me every morning before sunrise, and, in the course of the day, hurl at me all the swear-words they know.

All sparrows behave thus, but, just as the Madras crow is more impudent than any other crow, so does the insolence of the Madras sparrow exceed the insolence of every other sparrow, not excepting the London bird. I am not exaggerating when I say that the sparrows once evicted me from an hotel. I will not name the hostel, for I do not consider that it deserves an advertisement. It must suffice that the roof of the rooms occupied by me had in its structure a number of iron rafters provided with ledges. Upon these the sparrows held shouting matches.

And "what a dissonance is the sparrow's tone! Of all the Babel confusion of bird tongues, there are few more displeasing than this. All the boorish vulgarity of his nature is expressed in that tone!"

Well, I had to listen the whole day, not to one sparrow, but to a large colony, and, judging by the uproar, envy, hatred, malice, falsehood, deceit, and jealousy reigned in that colony. I was awakened in the morning—my first in Madras—to find that the crows had eaten up my *chota haziri*, and that the sparrows were fighting over the crumbs left by the crows.

Throughout the day those sparrows mocked me. In vain did I try to eject them. I flicked at them with a towel. They flew out at one window and in at the other, thoroughly enjoying the game. I continued the unequal contest for forty-eight hours, and then, having girt up my loins, betook myself to an hotel where the sparrows did not trouble.

The sparrow is no respecter of persons. He swears at crowned heads, treats viceroys with contempt, and gibes at bishops. Nothing is sacred with him. He forces his way into the seraglio and stares impudently at the unveiled inmates. He struts into the halls of justice, and there commits contempt of court He invades church, chapel, and cathedral, and, as Lockwood Kipling hath it, "perches on the organ pipes in full blast, and chatters loudly through the sermon."

One of his favourite pastimes is to sit on a beam under the eaves of the verandah and contemplate the human occupants. His stare on such occasions is equalled in impertinence only by that with which the cockney, spending Saturday afternoon at Hampton Court, annoys the occupants of the houseboats on the Thames. Doubtless, if we only understood them, we should find the personal remarks of the sparrow as insulting as his stare. Needless to say, the sparrow is not aware of his deficiencies. He thinks himself a mighty fine fellow. And in truth he is not a bad-looking bird, in spite of his squat figure, his coarse beak and vulgar tail. In England, one seldom has the opportunity of seeing the sparrow at his best, for there he is nearly always begrimed with soot and dust, but in India we can distinguish the smart grey crown that adorns his head, and his white shirt-front and black tie. The female is of course a homely-looking bird.

Where the sparrow makes a mistake is in imagining that he is a fine singer. Any one who could disabuse his mind on this point would be rendering a great service, not only to mankind, but to the whole of the bird world. This I fear is an impossible task. Until the end of the chapter the sparrow will continue to think that he alone of all birds can sing, and to look upon the vocal attempts of all other birds as impertinent imitations of his voice!

In this world one, or more, of three things are necessary to ensure success. These are ability, impudence, and a friend at court. Of the three, ability is by far the least important, and may, I think, be neglected. Impudence, on the other hand, may, without much exaggeration, be said to be the one thing needful to succeed in this wicked world.

Of this invaluable quality the sparrow has an inexhaustible supply. He is the most successful bird in the world. He is the most numerous fowl in Asia and in Europe. He has invaded America and taken the country by storm. He is the revenge of the Old World for the Yankee invasion. The sparrow has lately extended his kingdom to Australia and New Zealand, where he is now one of the commonest of birds. But for the fact that young sparrow is a dish highly esteemed by the crow, the whole of India would be brown with sparrows. Thus the crow is not an unmixed evil. But, in spite of his natural enemies the sparrow is a very fortunate bird. His impudence and "push" enable him to find food in places into which more timid creatures fear to venture. His very commonness is a blessing to him. It saves him from being caught and caged.

A sparrow, as such, has no market value. It is true that he is sometimes caught, painted yellow, and passed off on some innocent as a canary. But even when this happens his captivity is not of long duration. His happy purchaser takes him home and gives him a bath, when lo! the homely brown begins to show through the dye. This is a sad calamity for the owner, but a joy to the sparrow, for it means his liberation. His little cage is opened, and he takes to his wings, chirruping with delight to find himself free once more, and vows that never again will he be such a fool as to be caught by bird-lime.

THE NATURALIST IN A RAILWAY TRAIN

IN most parts of India a kind of "general post" of officials takes place at the commencement of every cold weather. The authorities seem suddenly to discover that the majority of public servants are stationed at unsuitable places, and thereupon seek to remedy this state of affairs, to the great profit of the railway companies. Having been an active participator in the latest "general post," I have been afforded an excellent opportunity of studying nature from the interior of a railway carriage. It must, in truth, be admitted that there are many worse points of view, for one sees an astonishing amount of animal life from a moving train.

The railway has now become quite an important factor in the life of many birds, chiefly owing to the fact that the iron road is accompanied by telegraph wires. When first erected, these caused the death of many an unsuspecting bird. The fowls of the air enjoy so vast a space, free from obstacles, in which to move about, that when flying they are not obliged to look very carefully where they are going. If a bird wishes to reach a certain place, it forthwith takes to its wings and makes a bee-line for its destination. Its chances of colliding with other birds are infinitesimal, it is not afraid of running up against a lamp-post, tripping up over a stone, or being run over by an omnibus or cab, so it puts down its head and lets itself go in much the same way as an athlete sprints a hundred yards race.

Thus it happened that when the telegraph was first erected many a feathered creature killed itself by coming into violent contact with the wires, which, for a time, were veritable death-traps. Calamities, such as these, are now happily things of the past.

Birds profit by experience. They have learned to avoid the treacherous wires during flight. They have further discovered that a telegraph wire forms a very comfortable perch, which that incomprehensible and eccentric being—man—has erected for their special benefit. Thus it happens that the traveller by railroad sees a succession of birds perched upon the message-bearing wires, as though they were sitting for their photographs, for the passing of the train does not perturb them in the least. A telegraph wire is, however, too attenuated to form a comfortable perch for some birds. For such there are the poles and insulators ready to hand, and of these the hawks and kites are not slow to avail themselves.

Birds which feed upon flying insects are particularly addicted to the telegraph wires, for these latter constitute an ideal point of vantage from whence the bird can look out for its quarry. Thus king-crows (*Dicrurus ater*) are to be seen distributed along the whole extent

BRAHMINY MYNA

BEE-EATER

of every railway, sitting on the wires until an insect comes within range, when the drongos at once take to their wings and give chase.

It is amusing to notice how the king-crow always seeks shade when the sun is very hot. In the middle of the day fully 80 per cent of the king-crow *habitués* of the telegraph wire will be seen seated quite close to a pole, so that its shadow falls upon them.

The roller (*Coracias indica*), or blue jay, as it is more commonly called in India, is another bird which is very partial to the electric telegraph. It sits indiscriminately on either wires or poles.

Doves, too, are very fond of resting on the wires. They are not insectivorous birds, and are, consequently, not on the look out for prey, but love to sit in the sun, especially in the early winter morning when the air is still chilly, and in this attitude they ponder over the problems which agitate the feathered world. The pretty little bee-eater (*Merops viridis*) is another frequenter of the telegraph wires. Very beautiful he looks in his green dress as he sits facing the line, and still more striking is his appearance when he makes a sudden dash at some Lilliputian quarry, for, when flying in the glare of the sun, his plumage assumes a golden hue.

The birds perched on the telegraph wire, although they absorb the greater part of one's attention, form but a small fraction of the species to be seen during a railway journey. It is no exaggeration to assert that a traveller by rail from Peshawar to Madras should, aided by a good field-glass, be able to distinguish fully one-third of the commoner birds of India.

The train passes through most kinds of country. It jogs along over barren *usar* lands, across fertile fields coloured emerald-green by the young shoots of the luxuriant crops, over broad rivers, past *jhils* great and small, through bushy jungle, amid long feathery grass, through forests, among bare rocky hills and green undulating down-like country. Each of these tracts has its characteristic species. Now a flock of mynas (*Acridotheres tristis*) comes into sight, chattering with delight over some newly-discovered field rich in food. These disappear and a pair of sarus cranes (*Grus antigone*) absorb one's attention. The sarus is a strange bird, which, like an Englishman, seems to take its pleasures sadly; it invariably looks depressed, although in reality it is perfectly happy in the company of its spouse. The crane and his wife form an inseparable and devoted couple. When one is taken and the other left, the survivor is said soon to die of grief at the loss of its mate.

Scarcely have these tall creatures vanished from sight than a flight of birds of a very different feather comes into view—a screeching crowd of "green parrots" (*Palæornis torquatus*) on their way to commit dacoity in an orchard of ripening fruit. The train now wends its weary way through a tract of marshy country, where, here and there, a paddy bird (*Ardeola grayii*) may be seen, lazily gazing into the water of some murky *jhil*. Near by are some duck and coots swimming on the surface of another sheet of water. Not far removed from them is a stork, and overhead are flying a number of white egrets (*Bubulcus coromandus*) and other *kuchnes*, disturbed by the noisy train.

MYNA

SPARROW-HAWK

Once again the land becomes parched, and a hoopoe (*Upupa indica*), Solomon's brilliant messenger, is seen making its way with undulating laboured flight.

And so interminable numbers of birds appear in rapid succession.

Nor are mammals wanting. These, of course, are neither so numerous nor so conspicuous as the birds. Apart from the domesticated animals, monkeys and black buck (*Antilope bezoartica*) are the mammals most frequently seen from a railway train in Northern India. The latter are now, alas, far less frequent than they used to be.

Writers of fifty years ago speak of the vast herds of these elegant herbivora which abounded in those days. Such multitudes are almost unknown in most parts of Upper India in this twentieth century. The companies are now few and far between, and so sadly have they diminished in size that a tiny herd, consisting of one solitary dark-skinned buck, surrounded by his little harem of fawn-coloured does, has become no uncommon sight.

As the grey mists of dawn are lifting, or when the sinking sun has become transformed into a great fiery ball, seen through miles of dust and smoke, jackals may here and there be observed sneaking furtively back to their "earth," or from it, on their way to help their comrades form a search-party which will presently render the night hideous by its unearthly yells.

The fauna of the railway station is not devoid of interest. There *is* such a fauna, for on this little earth of ours there is no nook or cranny in which Nature has not placed some of her children. Directly the iron horse pulls up, a crowd of kites may be seen soaring overhead, waiting for some scraps of food which a passenger will assuredly cast away. Needless to say, the crows are also on the war path, and, as they hang about, most impudent beggars, close to the carriage wheels, they get the pick of the food which is thrown out.

These bold birds, however, are not dependent on the charity of man; they help themselves, being obviously disciples of Dr. Smiles, whose book, "Self-Help," is so popular in India. A goods train loaded with sacks of grain pulls up at a station, and is at once invaded by crows, who proceed to bore with their powerful beaks holes in the sacks, through which they abstract the corn.

The enumeration of the fauna of the railway station would be incomplete without mention of the ubiquitous sparrow (*Passer domesticus*). Then there is the half-starved pariah dog, who is a regular institution at every wayside station, attending all trains. Experience seems to have taught him that charity is most rife among Europeans, for he usually takes up a position on the platform in front of a carriage occupied by them; but even their charity appears to be very uncertain, for his attitude is suppliant, he wags his tail in a half-hearted manner, he gives it the undecided motion that denotes hoping against hope. His ribs are very conspicuous objects, and the wistful look in his eyes makes one feel almost sorry that one's baggage does not include an assortment of juicy bones.

ROSE-COLOURED STARLING

THE CLOWNS OF THE FOREST

TRUTH is sometimes stranger than fiction, even in natural history. Thus Pliny, while he swallowed the stories about dragons and other fabulous creatures, refused to believe in the existence of hornbills. Later naturalists were obliged to acknowledge the occurrence of these "Rhinoceros Birds," but declined to credit the extraordinary stories that travellers told of their habits. Nevertheless, these stories contained more than the proverbial grain of truth.

It is, to-day, an established fact that, when the breeding season comes round, the lady hornbill is barricaded up in a hole in the trunk of a tree, and remains thus incarcerated until the eggs are hatched. In order that the female may not starve to death a window is left in her prison, through which the male bird feeds her. This extraordinary habit seems to run through the whole family of hornbills. The hole in which the hen-bird is plastered up is usually situated high in a lofty tree; when she has taken her place in it, both she and her husband proceed to close it up, except for the slit above referred to, by means of earth mixed with bird-droppings, or in some cases with droppings alone.

Here, then, among the hornbills, during the nesting season, is a division of labour as complete as that which prevails among human beings—the male goes forth and brings back food for his family, while the female stays at home and attends to domestic affairs.

How this strange habit arose it is difficult to imagine. Its *raison d'être* can scarcely be the protection of the female while sitting on her eggs, for her enormous beak is a weapon calculated to keep all raptorial birds at a respectful distance. It would almost seem as if the female hornbill is by nature a flighty young thing, a gad-about, and that consequently her eggs, despite the admonitions of her husband, used to suffer. She, no doubt, tried to do her duty, but the attractions of the gay world round about her proved irresistible; her spirit was willing, but her flesh was weak; consequently she and her spouse recognized that "durance vile" was the only remedy.

Many weak-minded human beings pursue a similar policy. I once knew a man at Cambridge who could not bring himself to take sufficient exercise to keep his body in health, so he hit upon the plan of starting out with three shillings in his pocket, and taking a cab to the railway station, which cost him two of his shillings; the last he used to spend on a third-class ticket to a station twelve miles out, and, once landed there, he had no option but to walk home.

I wonder whether any one has ever shot a cock hornbill at a time when his wife is plastered up in her nest. It would be a cruel but interesting experiment. What would the hen bird do when the cock failed to come and feed her? Would she stick to her position and die of starvation? Would she break open the barrier and thus put an end to her self-imposed imprisonment? Or would she sit at the window of her castle and endeavour to attract, by the "sweet melancholy" of her voice, some knight-errant of a hornbill? I have never had the opportunity of performing such an experiment, as, although hornbills are fairly numerous in Northern India, they seem very secretive with regard to the position of their nests.

Hornbills are caricatures of birds, freaks of nature, ludicrous clowns. There is not a single feature about them which is not comical. Mr. Wallace thus describes a hornbill nestling: "A most curious object, as large as a pigeon, but without a particle of plumage on any part of it. It was exceedingly plump and soft and with a semi-transparent skin, so that it looked more like a bag of jelly, with head and feet stuck on, than like a real bird." If possible the adult is a yet stranger object. The great hornbill (*Dichoceros bicornis*) is an enormous creature. It is over four feet long. Its great beak measures a foot in length and has a tremendous horny excrescence, known as the casque, which causes the bird to look as though it were wearing a cap.

What the utility of this "helmet" is to the bird no naturalist has yet been able to discover. Buffon thought that great injustice was done to the birds by their having to carry about this enormous deformity; he imagined that it hindered the birds from getting their food with ease! As a matter of fact, Buffon's sympathy was misplaced, for the casque is hollow, and so is almost without weight. During flight the wings of this hornbill, like those of most of its species, make a tremendous noise. Wallace compares it to the puffing of a steam-engine when starting with a train; that the simile is not exaggerated may be judged by the fact that a flying hornbill can be heard a mile away.

The voice of the hornbill is quite in keeping with the rest of the bird. There exist certain toys with which every one is familiar. Each takes the form of a clay figure representing some animal. This is highly coloured, and is placed on a miniature concertina. When the concertina-pedestal is pressed a horrible squeak is produced, which is apparently intended to represent the voice of the animal. It is only necessary to imagine such a toy over two feet in length, with a two-feet square concertina, in order to arrive at the voice of the Bengal pied hornbill, a bird found in the sub-Himalayan forests. When a hornbill talks it puts body and soul into its vocal efforts, its tail vibrates with each note, just as that of a crow does at every "squawk."

Hornbills have eyelashes, a very unusual feature in birds. This accounts in part for the knowing, comical look of the creatures.

It is needless to say that these birds cannot eat their food without buffoonery. They live chiefly on fruit, but they will eat insects, lizards, fish, and even scorpions; each morsel of food that is picked up is tossed into the air and caught in the huge beak!

Books on natural history state that hornbills are very shy, retiring birds. This has not been my experience. Recently, when I was sitting in a *machan*, waiting for a leopard, a pied hornbill alighted on the tree in which I was hidden. After having screamed a short solo, he caught sight of me, and although he was within three yards of my *machan* he did not fly off in alarm, but just cocked his head on one side and winked at me in the most familiar manner. I was not surprised; nothing done by a hornbill could ever surprise me.

When coolies are beating the jungle for game the hornbills of the neighbourhood usually follow the line, passing from branch to branch overhead, apparently enjoying the fun. These facts seem to negative the idea that the birds are shy.

The flight of the hornbill is characteristic. It consists of one or two rapid flaps of the wings, followed by a bout of sailing, with the wings expanded and motionless. Thus the line of flight is composed of a series of undulations.

Hornbills seem to be gregarious birds. They buffoon through life in little companies of six or seven. Fifteen species of these weird creatures are to be found in the Indian region. Of these, three patronize the "Bombay side."

MASTER IMPUDENCE

WHEN first I read Phil Robinson's account of the Indian squirrel I thought that the writer had painted the little rodent too black. That was in the days when I lived in Northern India, where the squirrel is to outward appearance a highly respectable animal. In that part of the world he rarely ventures inside the bungalow. Hence I used to regard him as a pretty little creature, half bird, half mammal, a four-legged denizen of the trees, a quadruped companion of the fowls of the air, a light-hearted inhabitant of leafy bowers.

It is true that I recognized that the squirrel was not sweet-tempered, that upon the least provocation he displayed "anger insignificantly fierce," that his voice was not beautiful; but these drawbacks were, in my opinion, more than set off by the fact that he is always amusing and pretty to watch. A stay in Madras compelled me to change my opinion of the animal, and to admit frankly that Phil Robinson was right when he said that every action of the squirrel, the very whisking of its tail, is an offence. I now regard *Sciurus palmarum* as the most impudent of all "the Tribes on my Frontier."

I am aware that many people regard the rascality of

the crow as unsurpassable. It is nothing of the kind. I verily believe that the average Madras squirrel could give the local crow its ten worst sins and then easily prove itself the greater villain.

When a crow invades the bungalow it does so with a more or less guilty air. J. K. Jerome says that only cats and Nonconformists have consciences; I think that the Indian crow should be added to this list. In any case, I have noticed that when a crow is about to commit a felony in my bungalow, he approaches it unostentatiously: he does not court observation, he will not commit the crime if he knows that your eye is upon him.

The squirrel has no such scruples. Even as I write one of those villains is actually committing theft under my very nose. He is perfectly well aware that I am watching him: he does not care two straws for that, he knows that, without moving, I can do him no harm, so he keeps one bright, wicked little eye upon me while the other is fixed on the food of my grackle (*Eulàbes religiosa*) or hill myna, as the species is popularly and incorrectly called. This bird has every day for its breakfast a plantain and a saucer of bread and milk. This latter is the object of the squirrel's designs. The nimble little rodent climbs up the leg of a bamboo table—there is nothing, by the way, which a squirrel cannot climb—and, having reached the cage, he inserts between the bars his two forepaws and thus abstracts, piece by piece, the myna's breakfast.

Strangely enough, the myna does not seem to resent the larceny. He sits on the perch and watches with an utter want of concern the barefaced abstraction of his property.

Now, I submit that, impudent as he is, the Indian crow would not invade my study and steal my bird's food while my eye was upon him. It is true that crows habitually commit larceny in my bungalow—theft in a dwelling-house is, I believe, the correct name in India for this particular offence—but they do so only when my back is turned or when I am sleeping the sleep of the just. Not only does the squirrel openly commit theft, but he glories in his misdeeds.

Yesterday I hurriedly entered my study and found a squirrel sitting on the table and chattering to himself at the top of his voice. I maintain that the most reckless crow would not dare to take up a position on my desk and proclaim the fact to the whole household by a series of loud and offensive "squawks."

What with the crows, the sparrows, and the squirrels, I literally have to fight for my daily *chota haziri.* The crows and sparrows attempt to steal only when I am asleep. The squirrels are bolder. When I am lying in bed awake, they creep into the room, climb up the leg of the table, and help themselves to the toast under my very eyes.

I sometimes sit up suddenly while Master Squirrel is in the act of grappling with a piece of toast that is reluctant to leave the rack. He bounds out of the room like greased lightning, and, as likely as not, upsets a cup in his alarm. When he is safely in the verandah, he turns round and abuses me roundly. Master Impudence never loses an opportunity of adding insult to injury.

But the language of the squirrel on such an occasion is as London milk is to neat whisky, when compared with what he says when "a lurking villain crow," who has been watching the theft from afar, pounces down upon him in the verandah and robs him of his booty. Then, indeed, is the wrath of the little mammal a sight for the gods!

It seems to me that the Madras squirrel is especially depraved. As I have already said, in Upper India the squirrels never, or, at any rate, very rarely, enter bungalows. It is true that in that part of the world the doors and windows are protected from the inroads of insects by *chiks*, but these are usually so ill-fitting as to form no sort of a barrier to a pushing squirrel. The fact of the matter is that the Madras squirrel is to the squirrel of other parts of India what the cockney is to the rustic, or the town sparrow is to his country cousin.

Colonel Cunningham bears me out in this. He states that in Calcutta they rarely invade the interior of houses, and he ought to know, for he lived there for thirty years. The Madras squirrel is as much at home among the rafters of a room or in the *punka* ropes as he is among the branches of a tree. He nests by preference in the bungalow, and, such are the ways of native architects and builders, that the interior of the bungalow furnishes endless eligible sites which are snatched up as eagerly as unlet houses in Madras at the beginning of the winter season.

Not being a dog in the manger and having no use for the various crannies under the roof, I should have no objection to the squirrels appropriating them for their nests if they did not expect me to find them building materials. That is the worst of a squirrel; you give him an inch, and he takes an ell; you allow him a free site for his nest, and he destroys a brand-new "Curzon" *topee* because he takes a fancy to the materials of which it is made.

Having constructed the nest with ill-gotten materials, Mr. and Mrs. Impudence proceed to stock it with young squirrels. The nest, I may say, is not much to boast of in the way of architecture; it is merely a mass of hay, wool, and soft fibrous material, in the middle of which is a hole. Here the youngsters first see the light. Two, three, or four are usually born at one time, and ugly little beasts they are. They are blind, and have not a hair on the body, but, curiously enough, the skin shows distinct signs of the light and dark stripes which are so characteristic of the adult.

It is, of course, a matter of common knowledge how the squirrel acquired his stripes. It was before the days of the British *raj*, when there were no bridges across the Ganges. Hanuman had to cross that sacred river on urgent business, and, no boat being available, the animals obligingly offered to make a living bridge for him.

Unfortunately, the backs of some, notably the porcupine, were not quite so soft to walk upon as could be desired, so Hanuman slipped, and his fingers, when he fell, rested on the squirrel's back and made five dark marks on it, which have since remained.

The beauty of the squirrel is his tail. That is a most

important organ. The animal does nothing without consulting it. Every time he utters his shrill, penetrating cry the tail beats time. A vibration of the caudal appendage is synchronous with every movement. It is also an index of the animal's state of mind. When a squirrel is enraged the tail performs wonderful gyrations. Jerdon says that "when alarmed the hairs of its tail are erected at right angles like a bottle brush." It is, perhaps, not superfluous to say, by way of comment, that the alarm in this case is that of the squirrel, not of the hairs of the tail!

Even the Madras squirrel has its redeeming features. Away from the bungalow it is a delightful creature—as playful as a kitten and as full of spirits. Two or three squirrels delight to gather together in an open space and there indulge in play. One will come up behind another and pretend to bite his tail, whereupon he upon whom the prank is played jumps high into the air and dashes off, followed by his comrade. After a little run, the first squirrel turns suddenly round and faces his pursuer, who then jumps over him. Hide-and-seek is another popular game with squirrels.

Sciurus palmarum is a much smaller animal than he looks. He is mostly tail, and so weighs very little. Indeed so light is he that he can safely trust himself to any branch that will bear a myna. Squirrels delight to crawl about bushes and nibble the more succulent parts. When walking along by a hedge one often sees a branch moving like a reed shaken by the wind, and, on approach, discovers that a squirrel is the cause of the movement. Most squirrels have a roosting-place or "dray" in some aged tree—often a tamarind or a banyan. As a rule they select a tree which is nearly hollow, of which the gnarled trunk is riddled with holes. Thus there are many entrances to the nest.

Usually quite a colony lives in one tree, and as the sun is setting the little mammals are fond of chasing each other about the tree, dashing in and out of the various holes in the trunk. There is such a tree in the compound of the Adyar Club at Madras, which the squirrels and the spotted owlet (*Athene brama*) have altogether appropriated. Before it is quite dark the squirrels retire to their lair, where they enjoy sweet repose until the sun again shows his face. They then emerge and bask for a little in his comfortable rays. The sun bath over, the members of the colony leave the tree, one by one, each to follow his own devices and desires.

KINGFISHERS

KINGFISHERS must be numbered among the commonest birds in India. They are fowl which observe Friday every day of their lives. They do this because they like fish. Quite a large number of the winged community subsist on a fish diet: there are the cormorants, the osprey, the fishing owl, and a host of other interesting fishermen, accounts of which would certainly fill a large book.

Three species of kingfisher are very common in all parts of India. *Alcedo ispida,* the common kingfisher, of course occurs; this bird is distributed all over the Old World. The variety found in India is much smaller than the one we see in England, and used to be considered a different species and called *Alcedo bengalensis.*

Naturalists, however, are now agreed that both the large and the small races form but one species. The difference in size is usually attributed to climatic influences; it is held that in the hot climate of India the bird does not attain its full devolopment.

With all due respect to those who entertain this theory, I would point out that the common kingfisher found in those parts of the Himalayas where the winter temperature falls to 16° F. in the night time is no larger than the Madras bird. Mr. Blanford says that this kingfisher is not found in the Himalayas. This is certainly not the case. I have seen dozens of specimens of the birds in those mountains at altitudes of 5000 feet and even higher. The common kingfisher has the typical build of the tribe: its neck and tail are short, its bill is long, and its figure distinctly dumpy. The breast is ferruginous, and the wings and back light blue, the blue of the former having a greenish tinge. The feet are coral-red. A white patch on the side of the neck completes the bird's uniform.

As it sits on a branch overhanging water, with its head buried in its neck, but bobbing up and down with spasmodic jerks as though it had a slight attack of St. Vitus's dance, the bird puts one in mind of a shrivelled-up Blue Hungarian bandsman dressed in a uniform three sizes too large for him. When, however, a fish shows itself the kingfisher becomes sprightly enough. It slips into the water at a considerable angle and reappears with its tiny quarry, which it first dashes against a stone and then swallows. The whole process is accomplished in about five seconds, and is performed with ridiculous ease.

No piece of water, which contains fish or crustacea, is too small to serve as a preserve for the common kingfisher. I once saw one sitting up over a pool, not three square yards in area, which had formed in a hole by the roadside.

A pair of kingfishers inhabit the Victoria Regia pond in the Botanical Gardens at Madras, another make the

COMMON KINGFISHER

Boat Club their head-quarters and dive off the landing-stage, a third affect the culvert at the tee of the seventh hole of the "Island" golf links; indeed, almost every piece of water in Madras has its special kingfisher.

Birds are essentially stationary creatures. The average non-migratory bird, if we except swallows and swifts, does not, under ordinary circumstances, ever wander more than a mile or two from what may be termed its head-quarters. Even migratory birds content themselves by travelling to and fro between their summer and winter quarters. A pair of kingfishers select a stretch of water and remain upon it until death parts them. They guard the fishing ground, when once it is selected, as jealously as a European power guards a new sphere of influence which it has established.

The common kingfisher is not a noisy bird. When it rests it rarely if ever utters a sound; when, however, it dashes along, just over the surface of the water, it emits a peculiar whistling call.

The next kingfisher which demands our attention is the beautiful white-breasted form—*Halcyon smynensis.* This is the commonest kingfisher in Southern India. He is one of our noisy birds, his unpleasant scream being one of the most familiar sounds in Madras.

He is distinguishable from the species already described by his larger size, his white breast, his more brilliant plumage, and the white bar on his wing, which is seen only during flight. Many birds have a similar white bar. The use of this to its possessor is a mystery.

In the case of gregarious birds, such as mynas, it is supposed to be useful as a mark of warning. One of the little flock sees danger and flies off; the flash of the white in his wings attracts the attention of his companions, and they follow him without knowing why they are flying away. But the white-breasted kingfisher is not a gregarious bird, hence in his case the white bar cannot have this meaning.

It has been suggested that it serves as a recognition mark, a mark whereby the male and female can distinguish one another from other kinds of kingfishers. This may be so, but it seems to me that, if the kingfisher has any difficulty in recognizing his wife, and I am far from asserting that he has, his difficulty would be in distinguishing her, not from a bird of another species, but from others of her own kind.

The white-breasted kingfisher is an organism full of interest to the zoologist, since it appears to be undergoing evolution before our very eyes. Those who do not believe in the theory of evolution—and there are still some persons who do not—urge as an objection to the theory that they see no signs of changing structure in the animals round about them; these are apparently fixed and stable, and not undergoing any modification.

It is true that Nature does not work in a hurry, that most of the alterations which are being effected are coming about so slowly as to be imperceptible to human eyes. There are, however, exceptions, and the white-breasted kingfisher is one of them.

The proper hunting ground for a kingfisher is obviously water of some description or other, but this particular species is often found far away from water. It is one of the common birds of our gardens, and is

found even in compounds which contain no fishing places.

I once saw a white-breasted kingfisher hawking insects on the Poona racecourse, just as you may see the "blue jay" hunting them on the Madras course. There is no water near the course at Poona. The fact of the matter is, the kingfisher is changing its habits. It finds that fishing is a poor profession, so is giving it up and going in for insect catching. It is becoming less and less of a fish-eating bird and more and more of an insectivorous one. It has advanced to such a stage that a sheet of water containing fish is no longer a *sine qua non* of its existence, as is the case with most kingfishers. Hence I make so bold as to prophesy that in years to come the white-breasted kingfisher will lose completely the knack of fishing; it will altogether forsake the water and obtain its living just as a roller does, and may one day even tackle snakes!

This bird can be kept in captivity. In 1900 Mr. E. W. Harper sent to the Bombay Natural History Society a most interesting account of some white-breasted kingfishers which he was keeping as pets. "Last summer," he wrote, "having obtained another white-breasted kingfisher, I determined to adopt a different method of feeding it. Small pieces of raw lean meat were pushed down the bird's throat, until, in a day or two, it took the meat of its own accord. This meat diet was varied with pieces of fish, the bird always striking its food (as it would have done a live fish) upon its perch three or four times before swallowing it. This was done with a jerking movement of the whole body.

"Lizards, shrimps, and grasshoppers are greedily accepted as dainty morsels by this bird. Although I have had the bird about nine months, yet I have never seen it drink. Its meat and fish are always placed in a jar containing three or four inches of water, into which it plunges its massive beak to take out its food. I might also add that the bird sometimes immerses its beak in the water, instantly withdrawing it with a shake of the head, even when not feeding." Mr. Harper adds, "the average weight of food eaten in one day is $1\frac{3}{8}$ ounces, or equivalent to about twenty-one minnows."

The third kind of kingfisher found in Madras is the pied one—*Ceryle varia.* The plumage of this bird is black and white, and has been aptly compared to that of a silver-spangled Hamburg fowl. This species is the finest fisherman of all. It looks for its prey, not while sitting on a perch as most kingfishers do, but while hovering over the water, and dropping into it like a stone when it espies its quarry. This bird has very powerful pinions, and will spend long periods on the wing without resting on *terra firma.* Now it hovers with rapidly vibrating wings high above the surface of the water, then it dashes off to a considerable distance, and again hovers; next it makes as if to dive; it drops, but suddenly checks itself, and flies off with a twittering scream, to hover again over another part of the water; perhaps this time it espies a likely fish and drops into the water, completely disappears for a moment, then emerges with its victim.

Some observers declare that this bird never dives without catching a fish. This I cannot believe. I have often seen the bird drop into the water and come out again without apparently having caught anything. It is of course possible that it may have seized some minute water insect and swallowed it at a gulp. Mr. Harper's kingfisher consumed in a whole day the equivalent of twenty-one minnows. That bird was in captivity, and did not take so much exercise as a free bird would; hence we may double the allowance of the wild kingfisher. If then it catches a fish every time it dives, forty plunges would suffice to procure it a day's food.

Every one who has observed the habits of this kingfisher knows that it dives very many more than forty times in the course of the day. It seems to hunt from morning to night. The birds are of course not always on the move. They frequently rest. One or two pied kingfishers are usually to be seen sitting on the telegraph wires which run across the River Cooum parallel with the Mount Road, Madras.

Kingfishers nest at the end of holes excavated in river banks. During the breeding season, which commences in December, numbers of nests, or rather the entrances thereto, may be seen in the banks of the Adyar River. The excavations are six feet or more in length, so that it is impossible to reach a kingfisher's nest without extensive digging. Nor are the passages which lead to the nest straight. But the nest is not much to look at. The white eggs are laid on the bare earth, and are mixed with fish-bones cast up by the birds.

Kingfishers, like most birds, object to having their

domestic affairs pried into. They will not actually attack the human being who tries to get at the nest, but they raise a tremendous hullabaloo. All kingfishers make similar nests. In some parts of India, however, the white-breasted form appears to be changing its habits as regards nest building, just as it is doing with regard to fishing. According to Mr. E. C. Steuart Baker, the white-breasted kingfishers found in Cachar do not excavate their nest, but build a roughly constructed one of moss amongst rocks or large stones.

Kingfishers are exceedingly unfortunate in having attracted the attention of the poets. Very few of these gentry can ever have seen any of the birds, but all of them have heard of them, and this they think sufficient to warrant their writing on the subject. Let me give a few choice specimens of what the poets are capable of.

Howitt writes of "the scarlet plume of the halcyon." We must, however, not be too severe upon this bard. It is quite possible that some wag dipped a sparrow in red ink and showed it to the poet as a kingfisher. The average poet seems to regard the bird as a sort of melodious seagull, having the habits of the bald coot. This the following quotations will prove:—

(1) "Bird of calm that sits brooding on the charmed wave."

(2) "When winter halcyons, flickering on the wave,
Tune their complaints, yon sea forgets to rave,
Loud winds turn zephyrs to enlarge their notes,
And each safe nest on a calm surface floats."

Phil Robinson, in the "Poets' Birds," quotes thirty equally idiotic effusions. But Shelley beats all records;

PITTA

no Yankee blood-curdling yarn-spinner could equal him.

> "Upon a drooping bough with nightshade twined,
> I saw two azure halcyons clinging downward,
> And thinning one bright branch of amber berries
> With quick long beaks, and in the deep there lay
> Those lovely forms, imaged, as in a sky."

Had he described a couple of kingfishers sitting on a merry-go-round, drinking ginger-pop and eating apple tart, the poet would have been equally near the truth. The worst evil one can wish to a bird is for it to fall into the clutches of the poet!

Eighteen different kinds of kingfisher are found in India, and a group of birds more interesting to the biologist does not exist. As we have seen, the white-breasted kingfisher affords striking evidence on behalf of the theory of organic evolution; the group, however, prove no less conclusively, in my opinion, the insufficiency of the theory of natural selection alone to account for the origin of all new species.

All kingfishers and their allies (except the aberrant form described above) have similar habits; why then the great diversity in their colour? We see in Madras the little blue kingfisher and the black-and-white species living side by side, each equally successful in the struggle for existence, and each carrying on the same trade; surely, then, if their colouring is due to the action of natural selection, both species should resemble one another in appearance. Yet as a matter of fact they do not.

What has caused this divergence? This is a question to which a satisfactory answer has yet to be found. Let us not be mistaken. I do not deny the adequacy of natural selection to produce new species. Undoubtedly, numberless species have arisen as the result of the weeding out of the unfit; but it seems to me that natural selection alone is unable to explain organic evolution. It is undoubtedly a factor in the origin of species and probably the most important factor, but it appears to be but one of many factors, several of which have yet to be discovered.

THE BLUE JAY

HE is not a jay at all; but the misnomer is perhaps a pardonable one, for in more respects than one the bird resembles the true jays, and I am told that the European roller (*Coracias garrula*), a near relative of the Indian blue jay, is known in parts of Germany as the Birch Jay. American visitors to India, however, make no such mistake. You never hear one of them call the roller a jay. They dub him the Surprise Bird, a name which admirably suits both him and the paddy bird, for when either takes to its wings a startling transformation occurs. The dingy heron is suddenly metamorphosed into a beautiful milk-white bird, while the untidy nondescript-coloured roller is transfigured into a gorgeous harmony of light and dark blue, into a bird flying the Oxford and Cambridge colours, putting one in mind of Putney on Boat-race Day.

Beauty is often a curse to its possessor; it certainly is in the case of the Indian roller. This bird has a wide distribution. It is, or should be, found all over India; but, alas! it is not. It is a significant fact that the bird is not common in the Presidency towns.

"Eha" does not even mention the roller in "The

Common Birds of Bombay." The bird is far from abundant in either Calcutta or Madras. A couple of blue jays live on the "Island" in the last-named town; but I cannot call to mind any others within municipal limits. It is not that the roller shuns cities and towns. Far from it. The bird is very common in Lucknow; I have seen as many as twenty of them studded over the *maidan* in front of the Oudh and Rohilkand railway station. Nor can we explain the rarity of the bird in Madras by assuming that the climate is unsuited to the roller.

The bird is common enough a hundred miles inland, and becomes rarer as one nears Madras. Any one who travels from Bangalore by the day train can verify this assertion for himself.

The truth is that European and American women are responsible for the rarity of this beautiful creature. It is one of the many victims of the abominable practice, indulged in by some women, of wearing birds' plumage in their hats. If this custom does not die a speedy death, all the most beautiful birds will, ere long, be swept off the face of the earth, in spite of the laws passed with a view to bird protection; for such laws are easy to break. Few can be aware of the enormous trade that is carried on in birds' skins.

Every number of "Bird Notes and News," the journal of the Society for the Protection of Birds, contains an entry similar to the following:—

"At the feather sale at the Commercial Sale Rooms, London, on 19th April, 1904, there were 161 packages of osprey feathers, of varying quantities, these

ROLLER-BIRD OR "BLUE JAY"

being all the plumes of the various egrets and small eastern herons, with a few of the common heron (*A. cinera*). Of birds of paradise from New Guinea, there were 3255, chiefly *P. apoda;* of Impeyan pheasants from the Himalayas, 648; of Indian rollers (blue jays) no fewer than 3913, with also a large number of East Indian pigeons (wings), and pittas, Indian owls, parrots, and jungle cocks. One firm catalogued 469 Chinese mandarin ducks. The remainder of the birds were mostly from America, comprising 52,628 humming birds, and numerous cardinals, tanagers, trogans, toucans, parrots, etc. There were also a large quantity of wing quills from pelicans, swans, geese, turkeys, and eagles."

At the June sale ten cases of peacock-feathers were sold, each case containing about 100 lb. of feathers. Thanks to the efforts made by the Society for the Protection of Birds, of which the Honorary Secretary for India is Mr. W. Jesse, F.Z.S., Meerut, United Provinces, many ladies now have scruples about wearing in their hats the corpses of little birds.

As an antidote to this, the "Trade" has started the fiction that "ospreys" are now manufactured artificially.

This has been more than once "shown up." It is not possible to manufacture such artificial plumes, and I hope that no statements to the contrary made by the feather trade will delude any lady into thinking the contrary.

But we must return to our blue jay, who, as we have seen, is no jay at all; nor is he nearly related to the jay family. The rollers constitute a curious little clan, isolated from all other tribes. They show affinities to both bee-eaters and kingfishers, especially to the latter. Indeed, rollers are the terrestrial counterparts of kingfishers: they are kingfishers which do not fish. Both families are clothed in brilliant plumage, and in each the sexes are alike. Both nest in holes, and both lay white eggs. These last two characteristics, however, do not count for much as evidence of relationship, being merely the consequences of similar habits.

It is almost a law of nature that those species of which both the cock and the hen bird are clothed in gay plumage lay whitish eggs and either nest in holes, or build covered nests. There are exceptions to the rule, which cannot be dealt with in this place. The reason of this general provision of nature is not far to seek. The hen, when she is sitting on her eggs, is liable to be attacked unawares by birds of prey; hence it is obviously to the interest of the species that she be as inconspicuous as possible, unless, of course, she be a bird, like our universal friend the crow, fully capable of looking after herself, or like the king-crow, a real fighter.

Thus it has come to pass that, in many species of birds, the hen is clothed in sombre plumage, even when the cock bird is arrayed, like Joseph of old, in a coat of many colours. It is, however, obvious that if a species nest in a hole, there is no necessity for the hen bird to be inconspicuous, hence among kingfishers, woodpeckers, rollers, and bee-eaters, which build in holes, both sexes rejoice in brilliant plumage.

Again, if a bird nest in a dark place, it is important

that its eggs should be as conspicuous as possible, for a bird cannot count, and if the hen is unable to see her eggs, she will not be able to tell when some of them get separated from the others. For this reason, it is my belief—but the belief is not quite orthodox—that natural selection has caused the eggs of birds which nest in holes to become white.

One of the puffins, which nests in a dark burrow, lays coloured eggs, and actually whitewashes them to make them conspicuous! This sounds as though that bird was a "real cute one," but I believe that the action is instinctive, that the bird does not know why she whitewashes her eggs.

Thus the fact that hen rollers and hen kingfishers are both gaily attired and lay white eggs, does not count for much as evidence of kinship. But in other respects they betray evidences of relationship. Both possess remarkably ugly voices. I have already dilated upon the vocal achievements of the beautiful white-breasted kingfisher, which is so common in Madras; I may now mention the fact that one of the Australian kingfishers has earned for himself the name of the laughing jackass. The Indian roller has a peculiarly ugly croaking note, and when angry emits "a grating cry or scream."

The members of both families are inclined to lead solitary lives. Although their food differs widely in nature, both families obtain it by like methods. Kingfishers take up a position on a rock, stone, or branch overhanging water, and sit motionless until an unwary fish comes along; then, in less time than it takes to relate, the little fisherman has dived into the water, come out again, dashed his prey to death on a stone, and swallowed the luckless fish.

The roller obtains his insect quarry in a very similar way. He takes up his position on the summit of a post, or on a railing, or a telegraph wire, and sits there motionless, pretending to be asleep. As a matter of fact, he is keeping a very sharp look out. Presently he espies an insect moving on the ground below, whereupon he flies to the ground and returns to his perch with the insect inside him. Both kingfishers and rollers must have marvellous eyesight. A roller will "spot" an insect in the grass twenty or thirty feet away and fly down and seize it.

The white-breasted kingfisher is, as we have seen, an example of a bird which is undergoing evolution under our very eyes. As generation succeeds generation, this bird goes in less for fishing and more for insect catching, so that now he often lives and flourishes far away from water, feeding almost entirely on insects. Hence his habits approximate very closely to those of the roller. There is, consequently, nothing wildly improbable in the hypothesis that, far back in the dim vista of time, there was no distinction between rollers and kingfishers, that the ancestral roller-kingfisher was a brilliantly coloured bird which picked up a living in a varieiy of ways, sometimes catching insects and at others fish, those that lived near streams naturally devoting themselves more exclusively to fish catching, and those which dwelt on the plains, far from water, contenting themselves with hunting insects.

Thus two races, having distinct habits, were formed,

and the kingfishers and the rollers proper came into being. It is necessary to say that the roller's diet is by no means confined to insects. The bird is not only able to swallow a toad, but to digest the unsavoury amphibian. A correspondent informs me that on two occasions he saw a roller devour a small snake. I have watched both kingfishers and rollers for hours together, and have never observed either species drinking. The former bird, when diving for his quarry, probably consumes as much liquid as he requires; but how does the roller obtain the wherewithal to wet his whistle? That organ must surely require wetting sometimes, especially in Northern India before the monsoon has burst. Perhaps he drinks on the sly.

This abstemiousness is not peculiar to the Indian roller. The European bird, writes Mr. W. J. Gordon, "would seem to be the total abstainer of the bird world, for we are gravely assured that 'it has never been known to drink.'"

Although we must admit that the blue jay sets a noble example to the over-ardent votaries of Bacchus, we cannot help wishing, with Mr. Gordon, that the bird would drink a little, if only for the benefit of his voice, which is very dry and thirsty sounding.

The Indian roller is sacred to Vishnu. It must be a very fine thing to be a sacred fowl, but I imagine that the blue jay would sell for a mere song its garment of sanctity. The bird must strongly object to being made captive, even though it be caught only to be liberated at the Durga Puja.

Four species of roller are found in India. One of these

is *Coracias garrula*, the European form. This bird sometimes visits the hospitable shores of Old England, where it is promptly shot by the bird-collector; but, as a set-off to this treatment, its appearance is recorded in the newspapers.

According to books on ornithology, the bird has been noticed in England "about a hundred times since it was first recorded by Religio Medici Browne in 1644." In other words, a hundred specimens of the bird have been shot in England, and probably not one in ten of the hundred slayers could have told you anything about the habits of the bird from personal observation.

Burma boasts of her own special blue jay, known to science as *Coracias affinis*. It resembles the Indian species very closely, and, were it not rank heresy to say so, I should feel inclined to maintain that the Burmese bird is but a variety of the Indian one. Certain it is that the two species interbreed freely.

Lastly, there is the broad-billed roller—a beautiful green and blue bird with vermilion beak and legs. It inhabits leafy forests and does not visit towns. This genus, like the other, exhibits local variations, and one ornithologist tried to make three species out of it, and had he been allowed to have his own way he might have made a dozen more; but the majority of zoologists stoutly resisted temptation. The result is, that instead of our having a number of species of broad-billed roller, so alike that it would need a committee of experts to distinguish one from another, we have one species only, which can be recognized at sight.

THE SWARMING OF THE WHITE ANTS

LAST night the white ants swarmed; to-day fallen wings are scattered in thousands over the floor of the bungalow. What a strange phenomenon is this swarming of the termites! It unfailingly accompanies the first rain of the monsoon, whether this comes in June, as in Upper India, or in October, as it happens in Madras. Scarcely is the ground thoroughly saturated with moisture when the swarms of white ants arise, apparently from nowhere; and, if they happen to appear at night-time, they make for the light and thus invade the bungalow.

Each of these myriads of swarming termites is provided with two pairs of large wings. Nevertheless, the insects appear to have but little control over their movements; their flight reminds one of the tottering of a child when first it trusts itself to its weak little legs. The wings are ephemeral structures; their possessors are given no time in which to grow accustomed to them, for they are used for an hour or two and then cast off to perish. Notwithstanding this, they are beautiful objects; each is exquisitely fashioned, every one is the work of a master hand.

Nothing shoddy is turned out in Nature's workshop; even organs which will be used but for an hour are finished with the utmost care. The mayfly, the winged life of which endures not a whole day, could not be more accurately constructed were it intended to last for a thousand years. The mollusc, that spends its whole life buried in the mud at the bottom of the ocean, secretes for itself a most beautiful shell—a shell which man does not see to admire until it is cast up on the shore by the waves, long after its possessor has passed away.

The birds and the lizards, however, care nothing for the workmanship of the wings of the termites. To them the insects are merely so many fatted calves waiting to be eaten. The day that sees the swarming of the termites is for the birds and the lizards a red-letter day, it is their *jour de l'an*, the one day in the year when they are provided with more food than they can eat.

Hagen tells of a swarm of termites in America where the insects formed a dark cloud, preyed upon by hundreds of birds, which so gorged themselves that they could not close their beaks! Yesterday the swarming of the white ants took place in the evening, so the lizards devoured the lion's share. Many of these reptiles must to-day be suffering from internal pains similar to those endured by many a schoolboy on Boxing Day. Tiny little lizards were to be seen running about the walls of the bungalow, seizing and devouring termites not very much smaller than themselves. They found the wings most difficult to negotiate, and most ludicrous did they look as they went about making frantic efforts to swallow the insects' wings.

If these lizards had possessed a little knowledge of natural history they would have deserted the walls and made merry on the ground among the termites that had already shed their wings. But perhaps it was as well for them that they did not, for had they been able to devour a whole white ant at a gulp many of them would, ere this, have suffered the sad fate of the King of England who partook too plentifully of lampreys.

By this morning all the white ants had disappeared as mysteriously as they came. Nothing of them was left, save a few hundred thousand wings. What has become of the owners of these wings? Many were devoured by lizards; some fell victims to other enemies; a few have lost their wings and apparently their way, for they are crawling aimlessly about and are being rapidly appropriated by the black ants, which are careering along excitedly, looking at each wing they pass, to see if perchance it have not a fine succulent white ant attached to it. When the black ant does alight upon a termite he seizes it with his powerful jaws and bears it off in triumph to the nest. But what has happened to the termites which have not been devoured? Surely all have not perished? These are questions to which it is not easy to give a satisfactory answer.

As every one knows, termites are not ants; they are totally different insects. They resemble ants only in that they are social organisms that live in colonies, of which most of the members are sexless creatures. The settlement is composed of a royal couple, whose sole function is to produce young, and the workers and the soldiers, who conduct all the rest of the affairs of the little nation. The neuters have no wings. The kings and queens are born with these organs, but lose them early in life. The winged swarms that appeared yesterday are the sexual forms; they are potential royalties; each has in it the making of a king or queen, if it can secure subjects.

At one time it was believed that the object of the swarming of white ants was the foundation of new colonies. It was thought that the winged creatures paired during flight or immediately after their wings had fallen off, and then each couple founded a new colony. This belief has been somewhat shaken recently by Grassi, who has made a prolonged study of the termites which live in Sicily. He declares that nothing comes of the flight, that it is utterly destroyed, that each component individual is devoured by some bird or beast; not one survives. Further, these winged termites are very silly creatures; they never make the least attempt to escape from the lizards which prey upon them; they sit still and allow the little reptiles to stroll up to them and swallow them. Fritz Muller laughs at the idea of a pair of these helpless creatures founding a new colony. As well, he thinks, place a couple of new-born babes on an uninhabited island to establish a new nation of human beings!

It seems to me that Grassi and Muller are mistaken. The swarming of the white ants must be of some use to the species, or it would not take place. If all the winged forms composing the flight were devoured by enemies, there could be no object in the swarming.

Philanthropy is a virtue unknown in nature. The universal practice among the lower animals is, Every species for itself, and the devil take the hindermost. Each species lives for itself and solely for itself. I find it impossible to believe that every year millions of termites take to themselves wings merely in order that the insectivorous birds and the lizards may over-eat themselves. These considerations alone seem sufficient to disprove the assertions of Grassi and Muller.

Not a few naturalists think that some of the individuals which compose the swarms return to the nests from which they emerged, or go to other nests, there to be received as kings and queens. This theory is very possibly correct, although it is not supported by any direct evidence. Indeed, there is the objection that in every colony of termites a few individuals are found which are known as reserve queens, individuals which, if suitably fed by the workers, will develop into queens. But it is obvious that such potential royalties cannot be produced indefinitely without the infusion of fresh blood into the colony.

It has further been suggested that these winged forms, although so helpless, may possibly contain stored up within them sufficient nutriment to keep them alive until some of the eggs they lay develop into workers. These, directly they are hatched, will feed and look after the royal pair. In support of this hypothesis we have the experiments of Professor Perez, in which he actually succeeded in obtaining some workers from a royal couple which were placed in captivity unattended by neuters.

Thus it is possible that some of the winged forms which appeared last night have been received into nests which are already established, have set up a new dynasty, and are to-day being acclaimed as kings and queens by thousands of loyal subjects. It is, further, almost certain that, of all the termites that showed themselves yesterday, a few couples have paired, escaped destruction, and managed to find holes or dark corners in which to lay eggs that will produce workers which will one day attack our property. But there is no denying the fact that the vast majority of yesterday's swarm have perished.

This enormous waste of life is a very common occurrence among Nature's humbler servants. In the case of some creatures it is probable that, of many thousand young which are hatched, only one, or possibly two, come to maturity; all the remainder are cut off early in life.

Nature knows two methods of maintaining a species. One is for the parent to give birth to thousands of young and leave these to fend for themselves as best they can, trusting that, out of the multitude, a few will reach maturity and in their turn produce offspring. The other method is for the mother to give birth to but few young and to tend these few with the greatest care, until they become old and strong enough to look after themselves. In the end the results are the same, whichever method be adopted, but the former is the more primitive one; it is the more wasteful, and suited only to small and lowly-organized creatures.

It may seem strange, seeing how numerous white ants are in India, that naturalists know so little about their life-history. The percentage of bungalows in this Land of Regrets which are free from these pests must be small. Almost daily do we discover some fresh evidence of their ravages.

Their latest exploit has been to devour the most savoury portions of my cricket-bat! Yet we know so little of their life-history. The fact is that the conditions of the life of termites are so peculiar that it is most difficult to watch them. They shun both light and air. They are creatures of darkness, and black are their deeds. Except for the short time that they possess wings they seem unable to live if exposed to light. They do everything in secret. They discover by some unknown means a decayed beam in the roof of the bungalow; the whole colony forthwith set to and proceed to tunnel through the wall from bottom to top. If perchance they come to a hard part into which they cannot dig, they go to the surface of the wall and there construct of mud a covered tunnel to hide their comings and goings.

They have soft, succulent bodies, highly esteemed as food by insectivorous animals; hence their fear of showing themselves. When taken out of the dark, underground world in which they live, they will do nothing, and, as the naturalist cannot observe them without light, matters are at somewhat of a deadlock.

There are supposed to exist nearly a thousand

species of termites, of which about one hundred have been described. Of the habits of three of these we have a fair knowledge. There is thus a large field of investigation open to any one who possesses the faculty of seeing through a brick wall.

THE PHARISEE OF THE JUNGLE

"That self-applauding bird, the peacock, see;
Mark what a sumptuous Pharisee is he.
Meridian sunbeams tempt him to unfold
His radiant glories, azure, green and gold.
He treads as if, some solemn music near,
His measured steps were governed by his ear,
And seems to say, 'Ye meaner fowl, give place!
I am all splendour, dignity and grace.'"

THE peacock has been the innocent cause of many a fight between the British soldier and the Indian villager. We can hardly wonder at a great desire on the part of Mr. Thomas Atkins to shoot the bird, for, as it rises laboriously out of a wheat-field, about four feet in front of the sportsman, it forms a mark which it is impossible to miss, and, when it has fallen, it is a grand trophy. Every feather of the bird is a poem of beauty. It is, therefore, not surprising that, in those parts of India where the bird is held sacred, the soldier sometimes overlooks the notices which prohibit the shooting of it.

The sacredness of the peacock is the one Hindu superstition with which I am able to sympathize; unfortunately the superstition is very local, and the result is that in the few districts in which it prevails the most gorgeous of Indian birds is fairly common, while it is a comparatively rare object in all the other parts of the country. The mischievous monkey is everywhere an object of veneration to the orthodox Hindu. One could wish that this superstition were more local and that of the sanctity of the peacock more widespread. However, we must be thankful for small mercies. It is well that peafowl are protected in some parts of the country.

The peacock is a typical Asiatic. His habits remind one of those of a non-Europeanized raja. He leads a lazy, useless life among the ladies of the harem. He lives for display. "The poor bird," said Chrysippus, "is created only for its tail." Had the Greek said that the bird was created for its train he would have been nearer the mark, for the tail of the peacock is a very insignificant affair; the train is formed by the great growth of the feathers which are known to ornithologists as the upper tail-coverts, since in most birds they merely cover the upper part of the base of the tail.

The gait of the peacock is pride personified. As he walks, his looks, like those of an oriental prince, seem to express the words,

"Ye meaner fowl, give place.
I am all splendour, dignity, and grace."

The beauty of the peacock has always fascinated Westerns. King Solomon used to import the bird from distant Ophir; while Alexander the Great sent one of these gorgeous creatures to Athens, where the people used to assemble in great crowds to see it.

The luxurious Romans imported the peacock as a table bird. It was served up in a dish ornamented by its feathers. This ingredient of the menu must have afforded the Roman cooks grand opportunities of indulging in a little sharp practice. I suspect that the same feathers used to do service a great many times and often ornamented dishes composed of game humbler than the peacock.

We are told that one Marcus Aufidius Lurco discovered how to fatten peafowl, and, in quite a short time, earned 60,000 sesterces at this occupation. In the Middle Ages peacock pie was a dish served up at every grand feast. The pie took the shape of the bird. The head and train protruded from the crust, and the beak was gilded.

Mediæval knights used to swear by the peacock. Later on men took to swearing by peacock pie. "By cock and pie, sir," said Justice Shallow, "you shall not go away to-night."

A mistaken, but widespread fancy attributes to peafowl very ungainly legs, of which the bird is supposed to be heartily ashamed. Solomon appears to have inaugurated the idea, and the rest of the world accepted it.

"The peacock," said a mediæval writer, "is a bird well known and much admired for his daintie coloured feathers, which when he spreads them against the sunne, have a curious lustre, and look like gemmes. Howbeit his black feet make him ashamed of his tail. And, therefore, when he seeth them (as angrie with nature or grieved for that deformitie) he hangeth down his starrie plumes, and walketh slowly in a discontented fit of solitary sadnesse, like one possest with dull melancholie."

A similar belief prevails in India. There is a country saying which may be thus rendered: "The peacock danced merrily until he caught sight of his legs, when he was ashamed and wept bitterly."

According to Lockwood Kipling, the supposed ugliness of the feet of the peacock is thus accounted for: "The peacock and the partridge, or, as some say, the myna, had a dancing match. In those days the peacock had very pretty feet. So when he had danced the partridge said, 'Lend me your feet and see me dance.' They changed feet, but instead of dancing the deceitful partridge ran away and never came back again!"

But let us leave these frivolities and return to sober science. Peafowl belong to that large family of birds which does not build nests. In such cases the young are born covered with down and usually in a condition to fend for themselves. The peahen lays her eggs in a hole scratched in the ground and lined with grass or leaves. The breeding season seems to vary considerably in the different parts of India.

The favourite haunts of peafowl are wooded, well-watered areas, but they often occur in cultivated country, especially in Upper India, where they are protected in many places. In such districts, at the harvest seasons, the birds appear to spend most of the day in fields of ripening crops, and dozens of them may be flushed in the course of an afternoon's quail shooting. Peacocks are very abundant in some of the groves attached to temples; such birds may be said to be in a semi-domesticated state. Indeed, peafowl seem to be as ready to attach themselves to man as their related species which have already been domesticated. It is strange that peacocks have not become popular pets. Possibly this is owing to the absurd English superstition which accounts peacocks' feathers "unlucky," whatever that may mean. Perhaps it is due to the fact that the bird has a penetrating voice, which is best described as that of a very lusty cat.

Unfortunately peafowl are prone to give the world the benefit of their vocal music in the dead of night. However, cats habitually do this, yet cats are popular pets among certain classes of people. In Upper India I have more than once been awakened when camping, and thought that I heard the cries of some one in sore distress, but found that I had only been disturbed by the conversation of a couple of peacocks!

These birds, whatever they may have been doing during the day, invariably roost in trees at night. In localities where they abound, it is possible to distinguish, before it has grown quite dark, great black things high up among the leaves of tall, thick trees; these are roosting peafowl. When camping in inhospitable districts, where one's *dâk* and provisions arrived only at irregular intervals, I have often been reduced to shooting peafowl while roosting, and then literally smuggled my victims into camp in order not to offend the susceptibilities of the country folk!

Young peafowl make most excellent eating, quite as good as Christmas turkey, but an old cock bird can give points as regards toughness to any *dâk* bungalow *murghi.* In addition to grain, of which the birds are especially fond, peafowl feed on young buds and shoots, insects and lizards. They also eat snakes, and hence are useful birds to have in the compound.

As is known to everybody, peafowl are sexually dimorphic. The male only carries the gorgeous train. The female is by comparison a bird of sombre hues. Darwin explains the beauty of the male bird by the theory of sexual selection, the preference of the females for showy husbands, while they themselves are not similarly arrayed; for were they thus resplendent they would be very conspicuous when sitting on their eggs, hence Natural Selection has tended to keep the plumage of the females of a dull, uniform colour. However, it seems to me that this theory fails to account for all the brilliant hues of the male bird, for all the wonderful markings on each of the feathers of his train. Nor does the theory of Wallace, that these are the expression of the great vital force, of the abundance of energy in which the bird rejoices. Animal colouration forms one of the most interesting of scientific studies, and it seems to me that explanations have yet to be found of not a few of the shades and markings which render the plumage of many birds so indescribably beautiful.

The science of animal colouration is in its infancy; yet popular books on natural history give one to understand that the last word has been said on the subject.

FLYING FOXES

EVERY one interested in bats should make a point of taking a morning ride along the Westcott Road, Madras, in order to see the flying foxes going to bed. In a compound within a stone's-throw of the Club are some tall casuarina-trees which form the dormitory of the frugivorous *Cheiroptera* of Royapettah. Since a bat has no clothes to take off when it goes to bed, having merely to fly up to a branch, catch hold of it with the hooks at the posterior end of the wings, and then let itself hang, the process of retiring for the night, or, rather, the day, should not be a long one. Nor would it be if these winged mammals were amiable creatures. But, alas! more cross-grained, surly brutes do not exist! It is one of the strangest freaks of Dame Nature that she should have granted wings—the emblems of purity—to one mammal only, and that the most unclean, loathsome, and ill-tempered of them all.

Some time after the sun has shown himself above the trees, and long after the fowls of the air are up and doing, the flying foxes begin to think of going to bed. These great creatures, the expanse of whose wings is over a yard, come sailing up from all directions, and, for a time, wheel round the roosting trees. After a little, one of the bats approaches a branch, catches the hook-like claws of his hind limbs over it, and allows himself to hang. When once a bat has thus taken up a position on a bough, he looks upon that particular bough as his own especial property, just as a human being appropriates a compartment of a railway carriage; but whereas *Homo sapiens* only stares angrily at another of his species who dares to intrude, *Pteropus edwardsi* not only glares at any other bat that makes so bold as to venture on to the branch appropriated by him (for bats are not blind), but attacks it with teeth and claws, and at the same time shrieks, "Why the deuce can't you keep out of this?" or words to that effect. The intruder then remarks, in a screech, that had he known the class of bat that was accustomed to hang out on that branch he would not have defiled himself by hooking on to it!

Having thus relieved his ruffled feelings he betakes himself to another part of the tree. Eventually, all the desirable boughs are occupied by flying foxes; but still many of the animals are without accommodation, and fresh ones continue to arrive. Then the real fun begins. Little tiffs, such as that described above, pale into insignificance before the squabbles which now take place. Each of those thousand odd bats has made up its mind to roost in one of those four trees, and each of those already hanging on is equally determined to have a branch all to itself. Hence the place becomes a veritable pandemonium, and the noise of the fighting and squabbling can be heard everywhere within a quarter-mile radius.

The best way to see the fun is to follow the fortunes of one particular bat. The other day I fixed my attention on one stout fellow who had taken up a position at the lower end of a bare branch at the top of a tree. The bough was at least a couple of yards in length and hence was obviously intended "to seat five." A few seconds after this bat had comfortably settled himself for the day, another came up and quietly hooked on to the upper end of the branch. The first comer immediately proceeded to abuse him roundly, and sidled up to him with great speed, in precisely the same way as a man, hanging by his arms from a horizontal bar, moves himself along by sliding first one hand and then the other along the bar. The intruder waited for him to come quite close up and then flew off swearing, leaving the prior occupant in sole possession. This individual then edged back to the lower part of the branch. He had scarcely arrived there before another bat hooked itself on to the upper end of the bough. Exactly the same comedy was acted, the original possessor again asserting his prior claim. But he had constantly to fight for it. Within three minutes I saw him drive off five intruders.

This is but a specimen of the kind of thing that takes place simultaneously all over the tree. Since bats appear to dislike each other's company so intensely it is strange that they always roost in large colonies, and invariably in the same tree. Possibly they do so for the sake of safety. A sleeping flying fox is a conspicuous object; and were he alone the eagles, kites, and crows might give him a bad time.

After about two hours' constant vituperation and fighting, things begin to quiet down a little. By this time it is probably long past nine o'clock. The quiet is, however, only relative; throughout the day the squabbling seems never to entirely cease; the whole colony appears to be in a state of stifled wrath, ready to bubble forth at any moment. Some of the bats seem to suffer from sleeplessness, and such individuals take good care that their immediate neighbours shall keep them company. A bat will suddenly, and without any apparent provocation, attack its sleeping friend. A fight of course ensues which, as likely as not, will spread; for a flying fox, like an Irishman, seems always ready for a row. Such fights invariably end in two or three individuals being jockeyed out of their places. The bats thus evicted seek new roosting-stations, and these become the centres of fresh squabbles.

Perhaps about 4 p.m. is the quietest part of the day; for by this time the bats begin to realize that the hour is at hand when they must be up and doing, so that it is a case of "now or never" if they want any sleep that day. The bat colony then looks like a number of dried cocoanuts hanging from trees—cocoanuts round the upper part of which a black membrane has been wrapped. This appearance is due to the fact that the wings and fur of a flying fox are not the same colour. The former are almost black, while the fur is of a reddish-brown hue. If the day be very hot, the bats hang by one wing and fan themselves with the other.

While yet the sun is above the horizon the early-rising members of the community awake from their disturbed slumbers, and make preparation for the work of the night. They take to their wings and fly about over the roosting-trees. Gradually they are joined by their companions who, one by one, spread out their leathery pinions; and soon the whole colony is in motion. The mere fact of flying through the air seems to put the creatures in a better frame of mind, for the discordant clamour above described is no longer heard. It is replaced by another cry, which, if not pleasing to the ear, does not set one's teeth on edge. The flying fox, as it sails through the air with easy motion, gives vent to a sound intermediate between the "quack" of a duck and the "caw" of a crow.

As the veil of darkness begins to fall over the face of the earth, the members of the bat colony cease from circling round the roosting-trees and fly off in various directions in long columns, each bound for some orchard or fruit-tree.

Flying foxes live almost exclusively on fruit; and greedy brutes they are. Each one probably devours more than its own weight of fruit during the night, and doubtless destroys as much as it consumes. Seeing that the population of fruit-eating bats within municipal limits must number several thousands, it is not surprising that one's butler is continually assuring one that fruit is difficult to procure in Madras. The amount of damage done to orchards by these flying foxes must be enormous. Indeed, letters of complaint have appeared in the "Madras Mail" from those who have suffered at the hands of the frugivorous *Cheiroptera*.

Jerdon is my authority for saying of flying foxes: "The flesh is esteemed good eating by some. Colonel Sykes calls it delicate, and with no bad flavour, and states that it is eaten by the native Portuguese. Many classes in the Madras Presidency also eat it." Arise, then, ye epicures who love to tickle your palates with the savoury flesh of these winged mammals, arise and make hay while the sun shines, for in Madras, near the Club, lives a whole farmyard of fine, well-fed flying foxes, only waiting to be eaten!

THE HOOPOE

NO garden is worthy of the name if it possesses not a lawn of emerald grass, soft as velvet; likewise, no lawn in India is complete unless it be ornamented by one or two hoopoes. Delightful birds, these, and as unique as delightful. There are no birds like unto them. Theirs is a profession of which they enjoy a monopoly. They are the only birds which habitually dig into the springy turf for their insect food. Snipe, sandpipers, and innumerable other birds probe the soft mud of river-bank, marsh, or *jhil* for their prey; the hoopoe alone is able to force its long beak deep into dry soil. The bill of the ordinary long-billed bird is soft and pliant; that of the hoopoe is hard and stiff.

The hoopoe, then, as regards its manner of obtaining food, is a kind of dry-land snipe. It is, of course, in no way related to the snipe; the resemblance of the beak in the two species is but the result of similarity of habit. The snipe wades in water, so has long legs; the legs of the hoopoe are very short, so short that the bird has to walk very primly in order to keep its tail from touching the ground.

Hoopoes are exceedingly numerous in India. It is

but necessary to betake oneself to any open space, preferably a lawn refreshed by recent rain, in order to see some of these charming birds. In case there is any one who is not acquainted with the hoopoe, it will, perhaps, be well for me to say that the head and neck of the bird are fawn-coloured and ornamented by a crown of buff, edged with black—a crown which, according to the Mohammedans, was given to the bird by King Solomon, in recognition of meritorious services! The wings and tail are composed of broad and alternating bars of black and white; these form a bold and pleasing contrast to the fawn of the head and neck: indeed, it is difficult to imagine a happier combination of colour and pattern than that presented by the plumage of the hoopoe.

One would naturally imagine a bird so clothed to be exceedingly conspicuous; but the hoopoe is not so noticeable as one would expect, for its colours harmonize with its environment. Yet it is a conspicuous bird, and, since it feeds in open places, is obliged to protect itself by means of a ruse when danger is at hand and there is no time to fly away.

"On the approach of a hawk or other enemy," writes Mr. W. P. Pycroft, "it throws itself flat upon the ground, drops its crest and spreads out its wings and—heigho! as if in obedience to the magician's wand, our bird has vanished; what appears to be a bundle of rags remains in its place." I myself have never seen the hoopoe act thus, but can well believe it does.

I know a parson who once did a similar thing. He was gardening, and was wearing the oldest of his old

HOOPOE

clothes (and that is saying a great deal, for his living was not a fat one), when he saw a lady parishioner driving in at the gate. With admirable presence of mind, the parson rammed his hat down over his eyes, stretched out his arms, and remained motionless in this attitude. The lady drove past him, learned at the door that he was not at home, and drove away again, little suspecting that the innocent-looking scarecrow was her spiritual adviser! There is, however, this difference between the parson and the hoopoe. The former consciously imitated a scarecrow, while the hoopoe's imitation of a bundle of rags is unconscious. It sees danger, is very frightened, and crouches in its abject terror. When it does this it has no idea that it is mimicking anything.

It is, I think, important to bear this in mind, because books dealing with mimicry sometimes give us the idea that the mimicry is conscious, whereas it is nothing of the kind. While the hoopoe is feeding, its crest is completely folded back, and looks like a prolongation of the attenuated beak. But, directly a human being approaches, the bird stops probing into the ground and regards the intruder suspiciously. If the bird be further disturbed his crest is instantly erected, and he flies away.

Seen from a little distance, the hoopoe is so very beautiful that one is naturally desirous of approaching nearer; but close inspection means a sad disillusionment. The cinnamon-coloured feathers, which from a little distance looked so soft and clean, are seen to be coarse, dry, and untidy, and here and there patches of bare skin may be visible. The full beauty of most birds cannot be appreciated except upon minute inspection. To this rule the hoopoe forms an exception.

Let us, then, content ourselves with watching him at a little distance. The crest of the bird, which was erected at our approach, gradually sinks, and feeding is resumed. Now, a hoopoe taking a meal always puts me in mind of a passenger hurriedly devouring dinner at a railway station. The bird feeds as though it were eating against time. It plunges its long beak into the turf with what appears to be feverish haste, seizes something, and swallows it at a gulp. It then takes a hurried step, and again plunges its beak into the ground. Besides excavating those insect larvæ known as "ant lions," which set traps for unwary creeping things, the hoopoe digs up each and every kind of subterranean grub. It also feeds upon ants, small beetles, and grasshoppers. The bird must have a most voracious appetite, since, notwithstanding the fact that it eats so quickly, it spends most of the day in seeking food.

Hoopoes live in couples, and usually feed in company. When they fly they sweep through the air in undulating curves. Most beautiful objects do they appear as their vibrating wings flash in the sunlight. They then look, as Colonel Cunningham well says, more like great butterflies than birds. The hoopoe, though it seeks its food entirely on the ground, is gifted with no mean powers of flight. Mr. Phillips states that a trained hawk almost invariably fails to catch it.

Hoopoes are pugnacious birds and are treated with great respect by their neighbours. Even the redoubtable king-crows dare not take liberties with them. The other day, as I was walking through a compound, I came across a pair of hoopoes feeding on the grass. A king-crow, which was perched on a tree hard by, made a dash at an insect and passed close to one of the hoopoes. The latter appeared to regard this as an affront, for he pecked savagely at the passing king-crow; the latter, having no mind to act as a target for the hoopoe, changed its course. Presently it had occasion again to pass quite close to the hoopoe, and the latter again pecked at it viciously. The king-crow then decided to go and hunt insects in a less dangerous place.

Hoopoes are, upon the whole, silent birds. They sometimes emit a curious little note, which Colonel Cunningham syllabizes as "ŭk, ŭk, ŭk, ŭk, ŭk." They can boast of no kind of song.

Like the common barn-door fowl and a great many other birds, hoopoes indulge in a daily dust-bath. Sometimes one may surprise them just before sunset rubbing their feathers in the soft cleansing powder which lies in a thick layer upon the less-frequented parts of the road. I have never seen a hoopoe bathing in water; I have an idea that the bird, like cats and Tibetans, and unlike Scotsmen, has a theory that water is injurious to the skin and should be only administered internally.

Both sexes are clothed alike, and as they are showy birds one would surmise that the hoopoe nests in a hole. This surmise is correct. The birds will build in almost any description of hole, in a cavity in the trunk of an old tree, in a hole in the wall of a house under the eaves, or in a hole in a bank. The entrance to the nest is often so small that it seems impossible that a hoopoe could squeeze through it.

But it is the feathers that make a bird; take away these, and what remains is but a fraction of the original. A sparrow will pass with the utmost ease through an aperture which is scarcely larger than a wedding ring. A hoopoe's nest is an exceedingly unsavoury affair. Any sanitary officer would unhesitatingly condemn it as totally unfit for habitation; but birds, like natives of this country, seem able to thrive in spots so odoriferous as to paralyse European olfactory nerves! The nest is just a bundle of rags, feathers, and rubbish, and has no distinctive shape or form.

Mr. William Jesse states that he once came across a hoopoe's nest into the structure of which a dead hoopoe had been worked. This is surely practising economy with a vengeance. Pallas states that he found a hoopoe's nest "within the exposed and barely decomposed thorax of a human body, with seven young birds just ready to fly, which defended themselves by a most fœtid fluid." It is in the face of facts such as these that I find it difficult to accept the theory of sexual selection, according to which the beautiful plumage and the magnificent songs of birds are due to the æsthetic tastes of the females.

Books on Indian natural history state that the nesting season of the hoopoe is from February to May. These limits, however, must be considerably extended. Last January two hoopoes brought up a family in an old tree in Madras. I further came across a nest in June at Gonda, in Northern India. The nest was in the mud wall of a stable, just below the roof. The nest is quite easy to find. It is only necessary to watch some hoopoes in the earlier months of the year, and, if they are nesting, you will be able to track them to their lair without difficulty. The parent flops lazily along, right up to the nest. It may feed the young from outside, or may enter the nest and remain there for a few seconds.

If you see a hoopoe visit any hole ten or twenty times in the course of an hour, you may be absolutely certain that it has a nest in that hole. Birds which nest in holes take no precautions to conceal the fact that they are going to the nest, as many birds, which build exposed nurseries, do. In the former case there is no need for caution, in the latter there is.

I have often amused myself by sitting quite close to a nest in a hole; the parent returns with some tasty morsel for the youngsters, and is disgusted to find an ogre sitting near the nursery. As a rule the bird will fidget about for a little outside the nest, in the hope that the intruder will take himself off, and, if this does not happen, it will boldly enter the nest. From four to seven eggs are usually laid by the hoopoe; these are pale blue or greenish white in colour.

Two species of hoopoe are found in India, but they are so similar that it seems unnecessary to divide them. One form is called the European hoopoe (*Upupa epops*) and the other the Indian hoopoe (*Upupa indica*). They are distinguished by the former having some white in the crest. But most birds in Northern India display more or less white, and these are regarded as hybrids between the Indian and European forms.

The hoopoes which occur in Burma have rather longer beaks than those found in India proper, so some species-makers want to form yet another species of him. The hoopoe frequently visits England and would breed there if it were allowed to do so; but the moment the beautiful bird sets foot on our shores it is shot by some collector, who then proceeds to boast about his exploit. The consequence is that the hoopoe is a very rare bird in England, and is likely to remain so until severe measures are enacted against that enemy of nature, the collector of birds.

UNNATURAL HISTORY: ANCIENT AND MODERN

IT is one of the most curious facts of history that, until quite recently, men, although they noticed animals and wrote about them, seem never to have taken the least trouble to observe their habits. In ancient and mediæval times zoological writers were perfectly content to rely on hearsay. They were not naturalists in any sense of the term. They were plagiarists, who did not profess to have even seen most of the creatures about which they wrote, much less to have observed their habits. Every writer in the Middle Ages copied largely from Aristotle and Plato, and incorporated in his works every traveller's tale he heard. No story seems to have been too childish, no occurrence too improbable, no exaggeration too great, no description too grotesque, to be credited by mediæval zoologists. Their bestiaries are crowded with animals that have never lived, while the accounts of those which do exist are altogether untrue.

Take the case of the races of men which, according to mediæval writers, peopled the various parts of the earth. The pigmies first demand our attention. Maundeville gives a graphic description of them; they are of "lytylle stature," being "three span long"; but they are "right fair and gentylle." They marry when they are six months old and live "but six year, or seven at the most." Next come the dwarfs. These are small men, but bigger than the pigmies. They possess the useful property of being able to live on the smell of apples.

Want of space prevents more than the mention of mermen and mermaids, crane-headed men, headless men, neckless men, noseless men, and men minus one or all the other organs. There were, also, one-eyed men, four-eyed men, tailed men. Then there was the hippos, the counterpart of the centaur of classical writers. The *monstrum triceps capite vulpis, draconis et aquilæ* deserves special notice, as showing the lengths to which mediæval imagination used to go. This was a creature with a human body and legs covered with scales, having three heads resembling those of a wolf, a dragon, and an eagle. One of the arms was that of a man, while the other was an eagle's wing. The finishing touch to this monster was a horse's tail!

As specimens of the creatures which fill up the mediæval bestiaries I may mention unicorns, phœnixes, cockatrices—the products of cocks' eggs—dragons, rocs—birds that used to amuse themselves by swooping down and carrying off elephants—basilisks, griffins, camel-leopards, and dozens of other grotesque creatures.

As has already been remarked, the ancients, even when they wrote about the birds they could see every day of their lives, made no attempt to study their habits or manner of life; they were content to relate all kinds of absurd stories regarding them. For example, it was universally believed that kingfishers laid their eggs on the sea, which kindly kept calm for a fortnight to enable them to incubate successfully.

The hoopoe was supposed to contain within it a stone, which, when placed upon the breast of a sleeping man, compelled him to reveal all the crimes he had committed. The pelican was said to feed its young with its blood, a supposition which any one could have disproved by casually watching the breeding operations of this bird. The death-song of the swan was another mediæval myth which has persisted even to the present day, for there still exist people who believe that a swan when it is about to die, sings most sweetly.

Not very long ago men imagined that to look a toad full in the face meant instant death! Even in this twentieth century there are plenty of writers of unnatural history. I remember reading, not many years ago, in an English daily paper, of a girl who, when she cried, shed the ray florets of daisies (the paper called them "petals"), instead of tears. The sea-serpent continually crops up, but we must pass over this important creature; we will not insult him by crowding him into the middle of a chapter.

Nowadays, most children are instructed in the rudiments of zoology, and are taught to use their reasoning faculties, so those who manufacture unnatural history have to proceed far more warily than they used to. They usually confine themselves to stories of unusual intelligence on the part of some animal.

There is, for example, the dear old "chestnut" about

the elephant, which every child is made to read. It will be remembered that the sagacious creature was taking a constitutional through an Indian bazaar. It happened to turn its trunk in the direction of a *dirzie* who was at work, and this individual pricked the elephant's trunk with his needle. The elephant passed quietly on. The next day it came strolling through the same bazaar and, as it passed the *dirzie* who had pricked its trunk, soused him with dirty water, which it had carefully secreted in its trunk. This is held up as an example of the way in which the noble quadruped revenged itself on its tormentor.

Let us suppose the facts are as stated—I am far from believing this, but let us for the moment suppose them to be true—what evidence is there to show that the elephant squirted water by way of revenge? If it did so, it would have to understand that tailors in white clothes dislike dirty water. Now, how could an elephant possibly know this? If there is one thing which it enjoys more than another, it is having water thrown over it; an elephant never loses an opportunity of dashing water over itself with its trunk, and the animal would naturally expect every other creature to like what it likes.

If one does a good turn to a small child who is sucking a sweet, that child will, if it be of a nice disposition, and not old enough to know better, probably take the sweet out of its mouth and offer its benefactor a suck! This it does, not in order to annoy the latter, but by way of showing its gratitude. So that, if the elephant did squirt the water over the tailor, it probably thought that it was doing an act of kindness.

Not many months ago, I read in a popular magazine of Natural History of some pigeons which took offence at something done by the owner of a garden, in which they were in the habit of feeding. The offended birds took counsel among themselves and then went away, and, having gathered together some other kindred spirits, proceeded to devastate the garden, uprooting plants and plucking the flowers.

The "Spectator" used to be a great disseminator of unnatural history. I am glad to be able to say that the paper has since mended its ways, and now publishes most excellent articles on birds and beasts by those who are really acquainted with their ways. As an example of what used to appear, let me quote the following, which has been republished in a book entitled "Cat and Bird Stories." The paragraph is headed "Feline Mourners." Says the writer: "A lady told me that there was a pet cat in her family, who was very fond of this lady's mother. When the latter was in her last illness, the cat was continually with her, lying on the bed. The lady died, and the cat was, of course, not again admitted to the room, though presenting herself again and again at the door. When the coffin was being carried downstairs, the cat happened to appear, and, on seeing it, uttered a shriek. . . . The sound made was entirely unlike those made by cats under any circumstances whatever, unless it be the cry made when in sudden pain."

Let us for the moment go so far as to suppose that

the cat was devotedly attached to the old lady who died, and that it understood the nature of death; we must further suppose, if we are to credit this absurd story, that the cat knew what a coffin was, could distinguish between it and any other box, and when it saw it, inferred that the remains of the deceased were shut up in it. Further, since the cat screamed the moment it caught sight of the coffin, it must have put two and two together in an incredibly short space of time.

Of all the disseminators of unnatural history the British poets are the most deserving of censure. Tennyson, Morris, and Sir Edwin Arnold are exceptions, but all the rest, as Phil Robinson rightly observes, "betray a systematized lack of sympathy with the natural world which is expressed in formulated prejudices."

The greatest calamity that can overtake a bird is to fall into the hands of the average British poet. No myth is too nonsensical to be swallowed by that worthy. The bards are quite content to echo all the absurd statements of the ancients. The bird of paradise has no feet, so sleeps on the wing, lays and hatches her eggs in mid-air. The pelican sacrifices her life in order to give her young ones a single meal. How the young fare after the mother's death, we are not told; presumably the father then "chips in," and after him the uncles and aunts shed their "life blood" in order that the young hopefuls may have a meal. The swan, of course, sings before death. Says Byron: "There, swan-like, let me sing and die."

All the other common birds receive similar treatment

at the hands of the poets, who are quite content to repeat worn-out fictions and to set forth absurd inventions. Few of them have any true sympathy with Nature, hence their works are collections of unnatural history. Nevertheless, they claim to be the "ministers and high priests of Nature."

British poets do not know, even, which are the commonest birds in the United Kingdom. If one trusted to them for one's knowledge of ornithology, one would think that every bush in England contained at least half a dozen linnets. As a matter of fact, the linnet is a rare bird. Probably, not one poet in ten has ever seen one except through the bars of a cage.

Pale blue is a beautiful colour. Cambridge is, therefore, the favourite university with the ladies. In the same way, the word "linnet" is very pleasing to the ears of the poet, hence his partiality to the bird.

THE GOLDEN-BACKED WOOD-PECKER

THE golden-backed woodpecker (*Brachypternus aurantius*) is the only member of the Picidæ family I have seen within Madras municipal limits; other woodpeckers may visit the city of Madras, but I have never seen them. If they do come at all, it is only at rare intervals; possibly the profession tax keeps them at a distance. *Brachypternus aurantius* is in its way a handsome bird. Its figure, it is true, is not beautiful, being workmanlike rather than ornamental. Its plumage, however, is as gaudy as the illustrations in the "tuppence coloured" picture-books of the Lord Mayor's Show, which are hawked in the streets of London on the 9th of November.

The cock bird has a crested head of the brightest crimson. The upper part of his back is rich golden yellow, which becomes olive-brown lower down, and black towards the tail. The wings are similarly coloured, except that the feathers are marked with large white spots. The sides of the head are white, relieved by bold black streaks. The breast and lower parts are black and white.

The hen bird differs but slightly from the male. She has the crimson chest, but the feathers of her head, instead of being tipped with crimson, are spotted with white. That so trivial a difference should be due to sexual selection I find it difficult to believe. The species nests in holes in trees; hence there is no reason why, so far as protection is concerned, the hen should not exactly resemble the cock in outward appearance. This is by no means the only point in the colouring of the woodpecker which needs elucidation.

Although the tribe displays a great variety of colour, no tint of blue is, I believe, ever seen in the plumage. Again, the young birds of some species are more gaily coloured than the adults—a most unusual phenomenon.

The woodpecker, being a highly specialized bird, is a perfect example of adaptation to environment. Its peculiar form is the expression of its unusual habits. Its beak is powerful, and is used as a pickaxe. With it the bird can excavate a nest in decaying wood, or dig out the insects which lurk in rotten timber. The bird also, by tapping its beak, frightens out of their lair insects which are hiding in the bark; and woe betide them when once they show themselves!

The woodpecker is provided with a chameleon-like tongue, which is armed with backwardly-directed bristles and a plentiful secretion of saliva of the "stick-fast" variety. The tongue is shot out at the insect with lightning speed, and in less than the twinkling of an eye the luckless creature is being hustled down the woodpecker's gullet.

One enthusiast thus describes the bird's tongue:

"It has the appearance of a silver ribbon, rather, from its transparency, of a stream of molten glass, and the rapidity with which it is protruded and withdrawn is so great that the eye is dazzled by following its motions; it is flexible in the highest degree."

Now, I must confess that my eye has never been dazzled in following the motions of the woodpecker's tongue, for the simple reason that it is unable to follow them, nor do I believe that any other human eye can. Imagination must, I think, be the source of the above description. I daresay if we could see the movement of a woodpecker's tongue at work it would look like a stream of molten glass!

Watch a toad, or even a lizard, catching insects, and what you appear to see is the *poochee* taking a voluntary jump into the mouth of its enemy. The insect, of course, does nothing so foolish. The motion of the toad's tongue is so rapid that the human eye cannot follow it. If tapping does not cause the insects to leave their hiding-place in the bark, the woodpecker drags them out by inserting its sticky tongue in the crevices. As the insects in question are mostly ants, I do not feel very deeply for them. The world can well spare a few ants.

The woodpecker's tail is not ornamental. As regards looks, it is but an apology for a tail. It is composed of a business-like set of bristles, which are very stiff and point downwards. But, ugly as they are, the bird could ill afford to lose them. They support it during its gymnastic performances on the trunks of trees. The breast of the woodpecker is flatter than that of most birds; this, also, is an adaptation to its scansorial habits.

Lastly, the bird's feet are admirably adapted to climbing. Its claws enable it to cling without effort to the smoothest bark. Some woodpeckers have four toes; our friend with the golden back has but three, nor does the loss of one appear in any way to interfere with its powers of locomotion. It can run up the stem of a toddy palm as easily as a human being can walk across the road.

The woodpecker is a tree-trunk acrobat. The bird adopts a unique method of progression; it moves in a series of jerks, just as a mechanical toy does, except that the movements of a woodpecker are as silent as the flight of a bat or an owl. Head, tail, and legs all work together, and jerk the bird whither it listeth. It usually progresses with its head pointing upwards, and can move with equal ease upwards, downwards, sideways, and in a straight line or spirally. The agility of the bird baffles description. It moves as though there were no such thing as gravity.

For gymnastic prowess, a woodpecker I saw the other day "fairly takes the cake." I was out one morning after a night of heavy rain and beheld a woodpecker disporting himself in the angle formed by the forked trunk of an old tree. The bird was dancing up and down like a jack-in-the-box, flirting his wings with each movement. I turned my glasses on to him and saw drops of water flying every time he shook his wings. The bird was taking a bath in the water that had collected in the hollow formed by the bifurcation of the trunk. He was bobbing up and down in the little pool, just as the orthodox lady bather at Margate does; but instead of clinging for dear life to the bathing-machine rope the woodpecker held on to the trunk of the tree.

Presently he ran a little way up one limb of the trunk, shook himself, and then jumped upon the other limb. This was quite a feat, for the bird's head was pointing upwards and his breast was, of course, pressed close to the trunk, both before and after the leap, so that the bird had to turn a complete semicircle while in the air. Then, after another dip or two, the bird ran up the trunk, hopped on to a branch, flew off, and was soon lost to view amid the foliage of a distant tree.

The woodpecker is not much of an aeronaut; his powers of flight are to some extent sacrificed to his tree-climbing propensities. His flight has been well described as "first a flutter, then a dip with closed wings." But this suffices to carry him from tree to tree, and the bird seems very proud of being able to fly at all, as he nearly always utters his laughing scream while on the wing.

The golden-backed woodpecker lays its eggs in a hole in a tree. It may either scoop out the nest itself or utilize a natural hollow. The bird has enough intelligence to make use of a ready-made hole, but there is a limit to its intelligence. Mr. William Jesse once found some eggs laid in the hollow of a decayed branch exposed to the sky; the bird had nevertheless cut out a hole on the under-side, although it was quite unnecessary! But we must not laugh at the bird for a little mistake such as this. Human beings sometimes do equally silly things.

A carpenter was once given an order to make a dog kennel to accommodate a retriever and her puppy. The kennel arrived. Although one-chambered, it had two entrances, a large and a small one. On being asked why he had made two doors, the thoughtful carpenter replied that he had made the big one for the mother and the small one for the puppy!

Woodpecker's eggs, like those of nearly all birds which lay in holes, are white. In such cases it is important that the eggs should be conspicuous, otherwise some might become separated in the dark from the main clutch and so fail to be hatched. Birds cannot count, but they can see.

There are fifty-six species of woodpeckers found in India, and all of these, with the exception of one genus, comprising three species, nest in cavities in trees. The exceptional genus, which is known to ornithologists as *Micropternus*, lays its eggs in holes made in the large ants' nests which are attached to the branches of trees. As woodpeckers feed chiefly on ants, their laying eggs in the nests of these insects is obviously a case of adding insult to injury.

But the *Micropterni* seem to be in every way disreputable birds. Blanford informs us that they have a "peculiar, strong, unpleasant smell," and that "their plumage is almost always smeared with a gummy substance derived from ants' nests, and the heads of ants are often found attached to their tail-feathers."

THE COCK-A-DOODLE-DOO

EVER since that far-off day in the prehistoric past, when some unknown Aryan *shikari* captured a pair of *Gallus ferrugineus* and domesticated them, the fowl has been the constant companion and friend of man. The utility of the hen bird soon rendered her indispensable to human beings, while the proud bearing and the valour of the cock gained for him the admiration of mankind.

Idomeneus bore on his shield at the siege of Troy a representation of the gallant chanticlere. The war-like Romans held the birds in high esteem; they were in the habit of using them as augurs. The method of ascertaining the will of the gods was to place food before the sacred birds. If the grain was consumed quickly, the omen was favourable; if, on the other hand, the fowls were slow in disposing of the victuals, the omen was evil. Since both cocks and hens have a habit of devouring their food as though they were travellers, determined to have their money's worth, eating dinner at a railway restaurant with the train waiting impatiently outside, it was not often that fowls gave an unfavourable omen. On one memorable occasion, however, they seem to have been off colour; the *pullarius* must have been trying experiments with them, for they refused the food offered them. This was too much for Claudius Pulcher, who was consulting them; he fairly lost his temper, seized the recalcitrant birds, and threw them into the sea, with the remark, "If you won't eat, you rascals, you shall drink!"

Our mediæval ancestors highly honoured the cock. Gerald Legh asserts that "the Cocke is the royallest birde that is, and of himself a king, for Nature hath crowned him with a perpetual diademe, to hime and his posteritie for ever. He is the valliantest in battle of all birdes, for he will rather die than yielde to his adversarie.' The cock, moreover, was believed to be able to impart his valour.

Porta writes: "If you would have a man become bold and impudent, let him carry about the skin or eyes of a lion or cock, and he will be fearless of his enemies—nay, he will be very terrible unto them." Extract of cock was held to be a cure for consumption.

The prescription runs: "Take a red cock, cut him into quarters, and put him into an earthenware pot with the rootes of fennell, parcely and succory, corans, whole mace, Anise seeds, and liqorice scraped and slyced, two or three clean dates, a few prunes and raysons." Then add half a pint of rosewater and a quart of white wine and stew the whole gently for twelve hours. A teaspoonful of the resulting broth should be taken twice a day.

The fowl, alas! has now fallen from his high estate, especially in India. In this country, although it is the true home of gallinaceous birds, the *murghi* is a very degenerate creature. Natives do not understand the art of breeding, as their miserably undersized cattle, horses, and donkeys, and their mongrel pigeons, demonstrate. Indian poultry, however, are worse than undersized; they exhibit a strong leaning towards pachydermism—a fatal creed for a table bird. This the traveller is able to verify for himself at any *dâk* bungalow, for *murghi* will inevitably appear on the table, and the would-be diner, after many ineffectual attempts to get his degenerate teeth into the bird sacrificed to him, is obliged to console himself for his unsatisfied appetite by singing gently:—

> "That bird must have crowed when they built
> the Tower of Babel,
> 'Twas fed by Cain and Abel,
> And lived in Noah's stable,
> All the shots that were fired on the field
> of Waterloo
> Couldn't penetrate or dislocate
> That elongated, armour-plated,
> Double-breasted, iron-chested,
> Cock-a-doodle-doo."

All the various breeds of poultry were at one time supposed to be descended from the common Indian jungle fowl. It is now, however, thought that Cochins and Brahmas have possibly arisen from other ancestors.

The Scrapers are a dimorphic family of birds—the sexes differ in appearance. The males are more showy and larger than the females. This is supposed to be due to sexual selection, that is to say, the preference of the ladies for gaily-coloured husbands. Each cock does his utmost to secure a goodly harem of hens. In order to gratify his ambition he must be of gallant appearance, of winning manners, and a good fighter. The former qualities enable him to obtain wives and the last to retain them when once secured.

The Rabbi Jochanan says: "Had the law never been given us, we might still have learned politeness from the cock, who is fair spoken to the female in order to win her. 'I will buy thee a dress,' he whispers in the hen's ear, 'a dress that shall reach down to the very ground.' And when the victory is achieved, he shakes his head solemnly and cries, 'May my comb perish if, when I have the means, I do not keep my word.'"

If the cock and hen birds differ in appearance, they exhibit still greater diversity in character. The cock is a warrior, valiant, careful of his honour, hot-tempered, albeit prudent, proud, and vain. The hen is the type of good-tempered bourgeoisie, humble, prone to cackle, subservient to her husband, foolish, and affectionate. The carefulness with which she bruises every grain of corn, lest it should hurt the soft palates of her chicks, the way in which she teaches her children to scrape the ground to make it yield up its good things, the tender manner in which she gathers her brood under her wings, and her anxiety and solicitude if one stray from her, are among the most homely and the sweetest sights in nature. But it is unnecessary to dilate upon the affection of a hen for her chickens; let it suffice that it has been made the subject of one of the most beautiful similes in the Bible.

Cruel man must cause the poor foolish bird many an anxious moment when he sets her to rear up ducklings. It is truly pitiful to watch her distress when the unruly brood betakes itself to the dreaded water.

There is a story told of a goose that saw a hen in this predicament, and swam up to her to cackle a few words of comfort. The hen seized the opportunity to jump upon the goose's back. The latter, although a little scandalized at the hen's familiarity, was too kind-hearted to shake her off, so swam with her alongside her duckling children. The hen enjoyed her trip so much that she repeated it the next day.

Then the goose, who hailed from Scotland, determined to float a company to take distressed hens for trips on the water at 2d. a—but stay! Methinks I hear the gentle reader complain of a pulling sensation in the leg. This will never do. Let us hie back to the young chicks.

It is characteristic of the Gallinæ that their young are hatched in a highly developed state, and not blind, naked, and helpless, as is the case with most young birds. The downy chick is so precocious a baby that it needs no nest to protect it, consequently the hen does not build one, but lays her eggs on the hard ground. While yet inside the shell the chick calls out to let its mother know that it is prepared to face the troubles and dangers of this life; then the excited parent breaks the little bird's frail prison by pecking at it. An opening is soon formed and the young chick emerges, ready for a good solid meal as soon as its mother has taught it how to eat, a lesson that is quickly learned.

Although born in so highly developed a condition, the

young bird differs greatly in appearance from either of its parents, and has thus to pass through a transitory, a hobbledehoy stage, before it assumes the adult plumage. Most birds live through this period hidden away in the nest, but the poor fowl has to do so in public. Hobbledehoys are always awkward, ugly creatures, and the pullet forms no exception; a more ungainly bird it would be difficult to find.

THE BATHING OF THE BIRDS

THERE is on the side of the Mount Road, Madras, near Munro's statue, a miniature pond formed by the overflow from a water-pipe. To this pool all the larger birds of the neighbourhood repair for bathing purposes. Every one passing the place, a little before sunset, will almost certainly see one or two crows, some mynas, and possibly a kite, enjoying an *al fresco* bath. It is a pleasure to watch the birds at their ablutions, for, while splashing about in the water, they are obviously as happy as the proverbial king.

Time was when scarcely a day passed on which I did not witness, from beginning to end, the toilette of one or other of the feathered creatures. That was in the Himalayas. In those mountainous regions water is a precious commodity during the greater part of the year. Deep was the sorrow of my *mali* that my little garden did not boast of a reservoir. Necessity, as usual, proved the mother of invention: the *mali* discovered an old galvanized iron bath, which he converted into a tank and placed in the middle of the lawn.

When I perceived the outcome of the gardener's ingenuity, my first impulse was to say hard words and issue peremptory orders for the removal of the unsightly tub. But, even while I shouted for the bearer, a myna alighted upon the rim of the bath (which was nearly full of water) and then proceeded to take a header into the liquid element!

I had never seen a myna do anything like this before, so a struggle took place within me between the naturalist and the artist; needless to say, the former prevailed. The bath was allowed to remain and disfigure the garden. In a few days it had become the recognized bathing place and drinking fountain of the birds of the vicinity.

The crows ruled the roost. When they came to bathe, all the other birds had to make way for them; for, in the feathered world, the strong invariably take precedence. Now crows, notwithstanding all their bravado, are not courageous birds. Nothing will induce one of their *corvi* to plunge into water beyond his depth. When it is a matter of bathing in one or two inches of water the crow is as bold as the famous Baltic Fleet. He will strut valiantly into the midst of the shallow pool, flutter his wings, and even duck his head in the water. But when it comes to a galvanized iron bath, in which the water may be eighteen inches deep, the crow behaves very differently. I never saw a crow brave enough to trust himself to the abyss of my bath.

The *modus operandi* of the bather was to take a firm grasp of the rim of the bath with both feet. He would then, still gripping for dear life, plunge his head and neck into the water and agitate them violently, and, at the same time, flap his wings and wag his tail. By

INDIAN HOUSE CROW

these means he would contrive to splash over himself a considerable quantity of water. Next, the bird would fly to a tree near by, shake himself as a dog does, and then begin violently to preen his feathers, dressing in turn all parts of his plumage, twisting his wings about in the most wonderful manner, and undergoing all kinds of acrobatic contortions in his endeavours to make his beak reach the more inaccessible parts of his anatomy. Presently, the crow would fly back to the bath, again duck his head and neck, and then return to the tree to resume the preening of his feathers. Perhaps he would go back to the water a third, a fourth, or even a fifth time, evidently enjoying his bath so immensely that he found it difficult to tear himself away from the water.

The mynas were more venturesome than the crows. They used to plunge into the water and disappear completely beneath the surface. But even they found that they had to summon all their courage before taking a dive. The bathing myna would perch on the edge of the bath and look for some time wistfully at the water, as much as to say, "Dare I?" just as a child will do before entering the sea. As a rule the complete immersion would be led up to by a number of half plunges.

The myna would hop from side to side of the bath; at the second or third hop he would allow the tip of his tail to touch the water. Then, with each subsequent jump, more of the body would be immersed, until finally the bird would do a *tout à fait* and disappear entirely. Having made this final effort the myna, looking very bedraggled, would fly off to a neighbouring tree in order to complete his toilette. Sometimes, when the water in the bath was low, so that a great dive of twelve inches was necessary to reach it, the would-be bather could not bring himself up to the point of taking the plunge. After much hopping to and fro, he would fly away, vowing, I doubt not, to take an extra good bath the next day, calling upon the saints to witness the fact that never again would he miss his bathe, no matter how low the water should be; in short, making all manner of good resolutions.

During the winter months the birds used not to visit the bath until the sun had had time to warm it. Birds do not like their bath water *quite* cold.

The bathing of the kite is a very sedate operation. It is accompanied by none of the splashing and flapping of wings which characterizes crows and mynas. The ungainly bird wades leisurely into the water and squats down in it for a few minutes. It then seeks some convenient spot and there remains motionless, with wings and tail expanded to the uttermost.

Kites may often be seen in such an attitude, face to the wall, on the ledge of the spire of the Fort Church in Madras. Vultures bathe in much the same way as kites do. They select a gently sloping river bank and enter the water to a depth of three or four inches. There they remain for a few minutes, sometimes motionless, sometimes sedately flapping their wings. They then walk out of the water, shake their great pinions, and stand perfectly still, until the sun dries their outstretched wings.

The smaller birds naturally require less water for their bath. Sparrows are quite content with a puddle. It affords fine safe bathing. The blithe little tailor-birds and the sprightly honeysuckers bathe in palm leaves, filled during the night with

> ". . . that same dew, which sometimes on the buds
> Was wont to swell, like round and orient pearls."

Fairy baths, these, and surely filled by the elf who cried:

> "I must go seek some dewdrops here,
> And hang a pearl in every cowslip's ear."

Other birds prefer a dust to a water-bath. The beautiful little bee-eaters bathe in this way, as does the hoopoe, and our friend the barn-door fowl.

When driving into the Adyar Club, Madras, you may, if you are fortunate, come upon two or three bee-eaters squatting with ruffled feathers in the dustiest part of the road, and rubbing their plumage in the soft dust with the utmost enjoyment. Then, after much preening of feathers, the little company of birds take to their wings and, uttering their faint little twitters, perform graceful curves in the air, becoming alternately green and gold with the changing angles of their wings.

There seems no reason why some birds should like water-baths, while others prefer *nettoyage à sec.* It is presumably merely a matter of taste. Some birds take both kinds of bath.

In addition to their ordinary evening bathe, most birds indulge in a shower-bath whenever it rains, and I think they enjoy this form of bathing best of all, provided the rain be not too heavy. They literally revel in a gentle shower. First one wing, then the other, is opened, the tail expanded, and the feathers ruffled in order that the soft water may penetrate to the skin. And when the rain is over, what a drying, what a shaking of wings and preening of feathers, take place! The bird world turns itself temporarily into a great Toilette Club. Then, the universal wash-and-brush-up over, the birds go forth on gladsome wing, looking as fresh and sweet as an English orchard after a shower in the merrie month of May.

BRAIN v. MUSCLE IN NATURE

NO observer of animals can fail to have noticed how they seem to lack brain-power. Judged by human standards, a bird or beast is but a stupid creature. If, however, we measure the other organs of animals by a similar standard, we shall not find them wanting. The adaptation of nearly every species to its environment compels our admiration. Some are wonderful athletes, others are possessed of marvellous strength, others exhibit incredible powers of endurance; in short, there is no physical characteristic in which some animal is not pre-eminent. There exist dozens of animals that are physically superior to man. But, notwithstanding this superiority, they are all his slaves, for mentally he is head and shoulders above them. Muscle is no match for mind.

Why is it that, of all the millions of animals, only one species—*Homo sapiens*—has "gone in for" brain development on a large scale?

Other things being equal, it is obvious that the animal with the largest brain has the best chance of survival in the struggle for existence. As compared with brain power all other qualities are of minor importance. If the legs of one antelope are half an inch longer than those of another, the former has certainly, other things being equal, an advantage in the struggle for existence. But other things are so rarely equal. A slight advantage, such as this, may be easily counterbalanced by luck.

Two antelopes may be feeding together, when they are seen by a beast of prey. They fly together, and the faster one soon begins to lead, but he happens to stumble into a quagmire; his neighbour profits by his mistake and takes another course, so that the poor creature who is floundering in the soft mud is fallen upon and devoured by the pursuer, while its less speedy companion escapes.

On the other hand, it is easy to see how a little extra brain-power can assist a species. A cute antelope may not be particularly fleet, nor very strong, but he will be careful to choose as feeding grounds places where he cannot be surprised, and, when he is chased, he will follow the course best adapted to his mode of progression; carefully avoiding all soft ground, he will profit to the uttermost by his knowledge of the locality; he will run, as far as possible, in a straight line, so that his pursuer will not be able to cut off corners.

Hundreds of athletic species, which are known to us only as fossils, might to-day be living, if, when the struggle for existence began to press hardly upon them, they had had the wit to build boats and sail away to some corner of the earth where the competition was a little less keen. Every organ of every animal is subject to variation, and the brain forms no exception.

How is it, then, seeing the enormous advantage in the struggle for existence which the possessor of a large brain enjoys, that natural selection has not developed more clever animals with large brains? How is it that all existing species are not as cunning as the proverbial serpent? Why is the average animal so lacking in intellect?

It is hardly necessary for me to adduce proof of this deficiency of brain-power among animals. Even Mark Twain noticed it; that humorist does not think much of the wit of an ant!

A pair of swifts once selected as the site for their nest the gateway of one of the colleges at Oxford. This was against regulations. So the college porter removed the nest.

The birds immediately began to build another on the identical site. This was also ruthlessly destroyed. The birds, with greater perseverance than intelligence, tried to construct a third nest in the same place. This was not obstinacy on the part of the swifts. They were unable to put two and two together; their brain-power was insufficient to enable them to understand that man objected to their nest being built on that particular site.

A dog is supposed to be an intelligent animal, but it will run away from a stuffed bear. An elephant, who is the wise man among animals, will actually pick up its own goad and hand it to the mahout!

But why multiply instances showing the limited brain-power of animals? Dozens of examples will occur to every one of my readers. It must not be thought that I assert that natural selection does not produce brain development among animals. It does. The crow is, in this respect, an enormous advance on the oyster. What I maintain is that, seeing the importance of the brain, we might have expected that this would have been developed in animals in preference to the other organs of the body. Yet it is the physical rather than the mental parts of animals which have been developed. Can we explain this phenomenon?

Herbert Spencer attributes the great development of the brain of man to the fact that he possesses a hand—an organ whereby he is able to appreciate space in three dimensions, and to understand the nature of solids. Every animal, which is not gifted with a grasping organ, possesses but a small degree of intelligence. This assertion, however, even if true, does not explain much. For we naturally ask, Why have not all creatures developed grasping organs?

It seems to me that the secret of the lack of brain power of animals lies in the fact that the brain is an organ which takes long to reach maturity, and which, in the early stages of development, is not of great use to its possessor. It is scarcely necessary to adduce proof of these two assertions. It is a matter of common observation that, long after a man begins to decay physically, his brain continues to develop. While we may take half a dozen new-born babes, who are potentially the cleverest men in the world, and set these upon an uninhabited island and they will surely die, in spite of their large brains. Dame Nature takes into account only the present value of an organ. She selects those animals which are, for the time being, best able to take care of themselves, best adapted to their environment. She pays no attention to potentialities.

If any one were kind enough to leave me a legacy of £1000—a most unlikely contingency—I should be deeply grateful, and think all manner of good things about that person; but if any one, in recognition of my services to mankind, were to leave to me, or my family, £1,000,000, payable one million years hence, I should not say as much as "Thank you." The present value of a cheque for £1,000,000 dated January 1st, 1,001,906, is *nil*. So is the present value of a baby's brain.

A tiger will not refrain from eating up a spotted deer because the latter, if spared, will develop into the cleverest spotted deer that ever gambolled in the jungle. Natural selection acts upon young and old alike; but it is the young developing creatures upon which Nature comes down with so heavy a hand; probably not one in a thousand of these reach maturity, upon an average. It is obvious that a most brilliant young animal may easily prove no match for the "old hand" of only mediocre ability. Hence the shortness of the period of helplessness is the feature most conducive to the preservation of a species—not necessarily a short period of development, but a short period of helplessness. Hence, in the lower forms of animal life, the young hatch out as larvæ, able to take care of themselves in the struggle for existence, or, if helpless, are protectively coloured to a marvellous degree. So long as Nature is hampered in this manner, so long as she is obliged to manufacture animals at express speed, she has no opportunity of giving her creatures a large brain, which takes time to make.

Millions of organisms which, properly speaking, have no brains, make a very fair fight in the universal struggle. A large brain, however, will greatly assist a species the moment it is fully developed. It is, therefore, obvious that, if Dame Nature can only hit upon some device whereby the young of a species are protected until they are practically full-grown, she will be able to develop in them large brains, and then that species will do wonders.

Nature has solved the problem. The solution is the evolution of mothers. It is obvious that if the full-grown members of the species can be made to protect and fight for the young ones, their development need not be rushed, they need not, so to speak, be hastily put together; time and care may be lavished in the making of them.

Hence the origin of the maternal instinct. The greater the protection given by the parents to the young, the greater the time that can be devoted to the development of the animal. It may be asked, if this was all that Nature needed—the evolution of mothers—how is it that, since this has occurred, all the higher animals are not as clever as man, or nearly as clever? The answer is that the maternal instinct, while favourable on the whole to the species, may be fatal to the individual; and if all the individuals perish, what is to happen to the species?

Animals with young are at a disadvantage in the struggle for existence. It probably has happened that many races of animals have perished owing to the excessive development of this instinct. The parents would not save themselves by deserting their offspring; consequently the whole family perished. Among most species the protection to the young afforded by the parents is so inadequate that, of the young ones, it is the physically strong, rather than the mentally powerful, that tend to survive.

One animal, however—*Homo insapiens*—in which the maternal instinct was highly developed, learned to take shelter in caves and to barricade the entrance to his shelter, so that the females were able to bring up their young without fear of molestation. There was then no need for the development of these to be hurried. The weakest of the family perished from disease and hunger while still under their mother's care, but the healthy children emerged, some years after birth, equipped with a large brain, so that they were able to overcome the superior strength of the other animals by craft, and the most crafty of insipient mankind survived and left offspring.

Thus *Homo sapiens* appeared upon the scene. He is the animal which pinned its faith to the brain, and his faith has not been misplaced. He has sacrificed everything to the brain. Almost all his other organs—his legs, arms, eyes, teeth — have been allowed to degenerate, but his brain has been kept up to the highest possible efficiency. He now reigns supreme over all the animals, which, so to speak, put their money on muscle, on brute force. These backed the wrong horse, and therefore are now the servants of those who staked their all on the brain.

THE KITE

> "Kites that swim sublime
> In still repeated circle, screaming loud."

THE kite furnishes a good example of what political economists call "place value." A kite nestling found in England will sell for £25, while in India the bird will not fetch even the price of the biblical sparrow. It was not ever thus. Time was when the kite was as common in the United Kingdom as it now is in India. Kites of a species (*Milvus ictinus*) nearly allied to the Indian bird used to exist in London in their thousands in the "good old days" when the conservancy arrangements were such that the streets offered plenty of food for carrion-feeders.

As civilization and sanitation advanced, the kites found that refuse, which is their ordinary food, was growing beautifully less, hence they had to resort largely to the farmyard and the game-preserve to supplement their more normal diet—a change of habit not welcomed by farmers and gamekeepers, who then began to shoot at sight every kite that came within range. Thus the species grew scarce. And when once this happens in England the end of that species is not far off.

The rarer the bird, the greater its value to the collector; hence every uncommon species is shot to extinction. The kite is now just not extinct in England. Its extermination has been prevented only by the fact that a few landowners have interested themselves in the bird and are protecting it. The kite, however, flourishes in the East, and is likely to do so for many years to come. It will be a very long time before India is Europeanized to such an extent that the kites have to subsist on poultry.

The kite (*Milvus govinda*) is one of the commonest birds in the "Land of Regrets." It is so very common there that it does not receive half the attention it deserves. Were it a rare bird we should marvel at its wonderful powers of flight. Indeed, the new arrival in India, if he ever notices natural objects, is perhaps more struck by the kites than by anything else in this country. Colonel Cunningham writes, after thirty years' residence in India, that he was so impressed by the kites that it seems only yesterday that he first saw them wheeling over the stream of the Hooghly.

I cannot refrain from quoting his description of them: "In truth, they are very beautiful birds. Their bright, bold, brown eyes and cruel talons are splendid objects; the soft shading of their plumage is admirable, especially when seen at a short distance, as the great birds glide gently to and fro, passing and repassing through alternate zones of sunshine and shadow; nothing can prevent their flight, with its easy evolutions, smoothly sweeping spires and headlong plunges, from being an endless source of delight to the onlooker."

THE PARIAH KITE

But, in order to fully appreciate the flying prowess of the kite, it is necessary to have been the victim of his larceny. You are perhaps eating a solitary breakfast, in the open, and your thoughts are far away. Suddenly you become aware of a presence, and a second later you behold a kite elegantly sailing away, carrying in its claws the mutton chop you were about to eat! I have seen a kite swoop down, snatch away a bone from between a dog's paws, and be out of reach before the dog had realized what had happened.

Mr. Jesse, in his account of the birds of Lucknow, writes: "On one occasion my *khansama* was walking across the compound with a bone on a plate when down swooped a kite and seized the bone, which, however, it dropped, knocking off the man's turban." On another occasion a kite carried off a tame squirrel from the shelter of its master's arms.

Well has Lockwood Kipling written of the athletic bird: "The kite is a notorious thief; no other creature is so splendidly equipped for larceny, for no other can snatch so unerringly and escape so securely." "When the kite builds look to lesser linen," says Autolycus. In addition to possessing marvellous powers of flight and accurate steering, the kite is able to use its claws as hands. It does not seize its food with its beak, as most birds do; it snatches it away with its claws, and, unless the stolen object is too large to be swallowed entire, transfers it to its mouth during flight.

It is interesting to compare the methods of the kite with those of its rival thief, the crow. When the latter bird espies something edible, he looks all round him to see if the coast is clear; then he hops or sidles up to the desired object, and, having again taken a look round, seizes the food with his beak. A kite, on the other hand, directly he catches sight of anything edible, swoops down and snatches it with his claws. If a crow and a kite "spot" a piece of meat simultaneously, the kite will have carried it off before the crow has finished wondering whether he can safely approach the object.

I have sometimes known a kite miss the object at which it was aiming. But this was invariably due to nervousness; the kite does not quite like taking anything from the hand of that mysterious creature, man. It feels that this is a risky operation, and resorts to it only when very hard put to it to obtain food.

Kites and crows live side by side, feed upon the same food, and obtain it in similar ways, thus it is but natural that the two species should not be on very good terms with one another. The crow is afraid of the kite. No crow will admit this, but it is nevertheless true. Often and often have I seen a party of crows squabbling over a piece of food; suddenly the fighting ceases, the crows look scared, and a kite swoops down and carries off, in its talons, the bone of contention, and thus acts the part of the peacemaker. Fortunately for the crows, the kite is itself not over-valorous, nor are its intellectual powers great.

The poet Spenser was not far from the mark when he spoke of "the foolish kite." In spite of its superior size, strength, and powers of flight, the kite is not infrequently "scored off" by the crow.

This happens mostly when the scavenger has dined well, rather than wisely. This, I regret to have to say, happens whenever the opportunity presents itself. Having gorged himself to bursting point, the kite likes to sit on the ground and meditate. A couple of crows then appear on the scene; one settles in front of the kite and the other behind him. The posteriorly situated crow then makes an attack *a tergo*. The kite turns savagely on the aggressor. This is the opportunity for which the front crow has been waiting; he attempts to remove one or more of the glead's tail feathers. After a little the irate scavenger flies off, amid corvine jeers.

Kites can scarcely be called birds of prey. They usually aim at more humble game. They are content to live on refuse. It is not that they do not like nice fresh meat; far from it. There is nothing that a kite enjoys so much as a tender little bird; but, before you can eat your hare, you have to catch him, and kites are lazy and cowardly. They choose the line of least resistance, and that is to pick up dead matter.

However, if a sickly little bird or a feeble nestling presents itself, the kite "makes no bones" about carrying it off. Sometimes the kite, in spite of the vigilance of the parents, manages to carry off a young crow. If he can get away before the parents discover what has happened, all goes well so far as the kite is concerned; but if the crows catch him red-handed, it is the very dickens!

Not many days ago the conversation of a *choto haziri* party, at which I was present, was interrupted by a great commotion overhead in a tree, and, looking up, we saw a crow abusing a kite. The kite looked at the crow in such a way as seemed to say: "Oh, you naughty rude woman! How can you demean yourself by calling me such shocking names?" And when we beheld all the fury of the crow virago we could not help sympathizing with the kite, who looked piety itself. Then we noticed that he was holding, under one claw, part of a young crow.

The other part of the unfortunate bird was doubtless inside him, and it was nothing but the mad fury of the crow, and the occasional feints she made at pecking the plumage of the slayer of her young one, that prevented the part of the crow nestling outside the kite joining the portion inside it. After having perceived the cause of the wrath of the crow, one could scarcely sympathize any more with the kite. Had any other bird been victimized, I should have experienced keen sorrow for the bereaved parent, but for a crow, no! All sympathy on crows is sympathy wasted. I regarded her, not as a sorrowing parent, but as Satan rebuking sin.

Interference on my part did not appear to be called for. Presently the kite flew off, carrying in its claw the remains of the young crow. The mother bird followed him up, swearing like a bargee, and, for all I know, she may still be giving that kite a bit of her mind.

The above episode renders it obvious that crows have good cause to dislike kites. The reason of the hatred towards them displayed by king-crows is not so apparent; but then drongos attack all birds. Sometimes the crows and king-crows unite in mobbing a kite, the individual differences of the two former being forgotten in face of a common foe.

A kite's nest is a very untidy affair. It is composed of coarse twigs, is sometimes lined with mud, and almost invariably contains a number of disgustingly dirty rags, some of which are utilized as lining for the nest; most of them, however, appear to be regarded as ornaments, since they are allowed to hang down and flap in the wind. Rags are by no means the only trinkets to be found in the nest. Brickbats, and, in Northern India, pieces of *kunkur* help to add to the beauty of the structure.

Kites usually build their platform-like nests in the fork of a strong branch of a tree, but they sometimes nest on mosques, temples, and old buildings. December and January are the commonest nesting months. A kite's nest is not a difficult object to see, being about three times the size of a football. The eggs are white in colour, splashed with red or brown. Two seem to be the usual number of a clutch.

I have already remarked that kites are not possessed of a vast amount of brain-power, and when nesting their stupidity knows no bounds. A Calcutta kite was once discovered trying to hatch a pill-box! This performance is, however, eclipsed by that of the kite which Mr. Littledale found sitting tight upon a hare's skull. One can only surmise that these objects must originally have been stolen as ornaments for the nest. But the kite, having a short memory, soon forgot the history of the foreign object and then mistook it for an egg.

Greater proof than this can scarcely be adduced to

show that birds during the nesting season are mere automata, creatures of impulse, driven by some inborn force to do many actions of which they understand not the meaning. The more one studies nature, the more does one become convinced of this.

"I once found," writes the American naturalist, Burroughs, "the nest of a black and white creeping warbler in a mossy bank in the woods, beneath which was an egg of the bird. The warbler had excavated the site for her nest, dropped her egg into the hollow and then gone on with her building." This conversion of birds into mere automata at the nesting season is perhaps the most wonderful phenomenon in nature.

It is obvious that if birds did not, at certain seasons, throw intelligence to the winds and become mere automata they would neither build nests nor sit on the eggs they laid. A bird which has never seen a nest, one, for example, which was hatched out in an incubator, will at the appointed time build a nest of the usual pattern, yet such a bird has had no experience to guide her. When, therefore, a bird sets itself for the first time to collect materials and to weave them into a nest, it is not consciously making a nursery for its chicks, it cannot know why it is collecting sticks. It probably never puts this question to itself. It is content to obey blindly an impulse planted in it by Him who watches over the little birds, and teaches them how to hold their own in the struggle for existence.

THE BRAHMINY KITE

THE Brahminy kite (*Haliastur lindus*) is a puzzle to naturalists. Its habits are obviously those of a kite, but it looks too fine a bird to be a scavenger; it seems too well dressed to be a performer of Nature's dirty work. Hence the bird used formerly to be placed among the sea-eagles.

Nowadays, naturalists seem inclined to dethrone it from its former high position, to regard it as an ass in a lion's skin, and to declare that, although it has the colour of the eagle, which, according to Shelley, "sits in the light of its golden wings," it is but a scavenger. However, the question is not yet decided. One is at liberty to regard the bird, either as a degraded eagle, or a glorified kite. Blanford declines to commit himself, and in this he is perhaps wise. He says: "*Haliastur* has been classed alternatively with the sea-eagles and with the kites, and is allied to both."

But the systematic position of the bird is after all not a matter of great importance. Let us leave ornithologists to squabble over this, while we take a look at the bird and study it as it is.

It is one of the commonest birds in Madras. Let me

say, for the benefit of those unacquainted with it, that the general hue of its plumage is a bright, rich chestnut, but its head, neck, lower parts, and the tip of its tail, are white. Each white feather has a brown shaft, but this is not visible except at close quarters. From a distance the bird appears chestnut in colour, with a snowy head and breast. Such is the adult creature; but it is not until the young Brahminy kite is nearly a year old that it assumes this beautiful plumage.

When it first leaves the nest, early in the year, it is a dingy brown bird, and, although it undergoes a number of changes in appearance, it remains a brown bird until the winter. Hence young Brahminy kites often pass for the common pariah bird. However, nothing is easier than to distinguish the two species, no matter in what stage of plumage. The tail of the pariah kite is more or less forked, the two outer feathers on each side being a trifle longer than the inner feathers. The tail of the Brahminy kite is fan-shaped. It is nicely rounded off, the outer feathers being slightly shorter than the inner ones.

In general habits the Brahminy very closely resembles the common kite. Both birds are gifted with wonderful powers of flight. They will remain on the wing for hours, soaring high above the earth, with but an occasional movement of the wing.

On one occasion I watched a Brahminy kite circling over the River Cooum at Madras. For fully five minutes the bird did not once flap its wings, yet it was moving the whole time. The wind furnished the motor power, and a slight depression of the wing, or a twist of the tail,

BRAHMINY KITE

sufficed to guide the bird. Thus it circled round and round, without effort, looking for its prey. Brahminy kites seem, like their vulgar relatives, to be almost omnivorous. They pick their food off the water by preference, while the common kites hunt over dry land. Thus the two species may be said to divide the land and water between them; but, unfortunately for the peace of the community, each frequently encroaches on the preserve of the other; this leads to a considerable amount of mutual abuse, which takes the form of squeals.

Some authorities declare that the Brahminy kite lives chiefly upon insects. This is not so; the bird will devour insects, as it will eat most things, but it lives chiefly upon garbage, which it finds floating on the water, and on frogs and crabs, which abound in paddy-fields. Numberless Brahminies are seen when one is out snipe-shooting near Madras, and these birds make no bones about carrying off a wounded snipe if they are given half a chance. On one occasion, when I was shooting duck, one of these kites made off with a teal that I had wounded. I fired at him to punish him for his impudence, but he flew off, apparently unscathed, carrying his quarry.

Some naturalists declare that *Haliastur* catches fish, much as an osprey or fishing-eagle does. Thus Colonel Sykes says: "It occasionally dips entirely under water, appearing to rise again with difficulty." I do not believe that the bird ever does this; the worthy Colonel must have mistaken some other species for a Brahminy kite upon this occasion.

The bird, however, does sometimes (very rarely I think) snatch with its claws a small fish or a prawn that is swimming near the surface of the water. Colonel Cunningham thus describes some fishing operations which he witnessed on a pond that had, owing to the drought, become very shallow :—"For several days the numbers of arrivals steadily increased, so that for a time the neighbourhood of the pond was thronged by hundreds of birds in various stages of plumage, and filling the air with clamorous cries as they flew in bewildering mazes over the water, or sat among the branches of all the surrounding trees. Every now and then one of the moving crowd would suddenly stop to sweep along over the surface of the pond, and rise again, grasping a little glittering fish, which he either carried off to be devoured at leisure on a tree, or disposed of while on the wing, just as common kites do when hawking in a swarm of white ants." Such sights are not seen every day.

Another observer witnessed "a Brahminy kite kill and eat a kingfisher that had carried off a small fish on which the kite was in the act of swooping." Truly there were giants in those days!

Brahminy kites sometimes come into collision with the crows; but then, what bird or beast does not do this? In Madras the crows treat their larger neighbours with great respect, having no liking for the feel of their powerful claws. But in places where Brahminy kites are uncommon birds, the crows mob them, as they do all strange birds.

Crows are very conservative. They hate any new

addition to the local fauna, and they show their dislike in no uncertain way, as a cockatoo, which recently escaped from captivity in Madras, discovered. The Brahminy kite is very fond of hearing its own voice, which is best described as a disagreeable squeal. It is uttered while the bird is on the wing.

The nest is built high up in a tree, often a palm-tree. It is not much of a structure if regarded from an architectural point of view; nevertheless, it is less bulky and less untidy than the nursery of its plebeian cousin, the pariah kite. It is composed of sticks roughly put together and lined with leaves or mud. The eggs are dirty white, sometimes splotched or speckled with reddish brown. The Brahminy kite rejoices in a great variety of names. Many Anglo-Indians call it the fish-hawk. Mr. Thomas Atkins calls it the bramley kite, which is his way of pronouncing Brahminy kite!

The Mohammedan name for the bird is *Ru-Mubarik*, which, being translated, means "lucky face." The bird is so called from a superstition that, when two armies are about to enter into an engagement, the appearance of one of these auspicious birds over the head of either of the armies means victory to that side. Now, since there must be quite a dozen Brahminy kites hovering over every army in the field in India, each side should always go into battle feeling cocksure of success. *Garuda* is the Hindu name for the bird, which is sacred to Vishnu. That god selected the bird as his vehicle, and it would be impossible to imagine a finer steed; but the bird, of course, is not up to weight.

Mr. P. V. Trivikrama Rau writes in the "Calcutta

Review": "Whenever *Garuda*, the vehicle of Vishnu, is seen, Hindus pay their veneration to it by touching their cheeks with their fingers as they repeat a Sanskrit verse which, when rendered into English, is as follows: 'I bow to thee, king of birds, and (as such) the vehicle of Vishnu, whose parts are coloured crimson and whose neck is bright as the moon.'" Now, I presume that Mr. Trivikrama Rau is here indulging in a little Oriental hyperbole.

It would be all very well for the pious Hindu to act thus when he lives in a place where one only sees a Brahminy kite once in a blue moon, but it is surely expecting too much of the Madras Hindu to do all this whenever he sets eyes on one of these birds. Every one in Madras must see dozens of Brahminy kites daily, and I cannot bring myself to believe that he does and says all the above every time he beholds one. Mr. Trivikrama Rau also tells us that the sight of a Brahminy kite "on any day, and particularly on Sunday mornings, is considered lucky, for it is believed that it is then returning from Vishnu, whom it has gone to see on the previous evening." The Madras Hindus are certainly in luck's way, for every one of them may depend on seeing a dozen or more Brahminy kites every Sunday morning throughout the year.

A CURIOUS TRAIT IN ANIMAL CHARACTER

INTENSE dislike of all strange objects that live and move is a characteristic common to all species of animals which are sufficiently organized to have likes and dislikes. In man the characteristic is seen in the hatred of foreigners which prevails among savage and partially civilized races. When the heathen Chinee tries to keep the "foreign devil" out of his country, he is merely giving expression to a feeling which he has inherited from his animal ancestors—the hatred of strange species.

The savage, when he sets upon and slays the white man who ventures into his domain, is but giving rather more forcible expression to the same feeling. The London street-boys, when they follow and shout out after any person displaying some peculiarity of dress, are doing much what gregarious animals do when a strange species suddenly appears in their midst.

A mammal or a bird regards every other species with which it is acquainted either with intensely hostile feelings or with supreme indifference. When it is suddenly confronted with a strange new species it is, for the moment, nonplussed. It, however, gives itself the benefit of the doubt, sets down the new creature as hostile, and acts accordingly. If it be small or weak, it makes itself scarce when it catches sight of the stranger; but if it be strong or gregarious, it forthwith proceeds to mob the intruder. The Indian crow, being a bold, powerful bird of gregarious habits, is an excellent subject upon which to study the feelings excited in an animal by a strange species.

Recently there arose a tremendous commotion among the crows in the fort at Madras. I looked out of the window to see what had happened, and observed a large white object flit by, followed by a mob of excited crows. The white object settled in a tree and I then saw that it was a cockatoo, which had evidently escaped from captivity. Its pursuers all perched in the tree, as close to it as discretion permitted. Their clamours filled the air.

The cockatoo thought that the summit of the tree would be a better strategic position, so climbed up to the topmost branch, with the twenty or thirty crows in attendance. None of them seemed to care to commence the attack. One or two made feints, but a threatening snap by the cockatoo caused them to desist. So the cockatoo and the crows remained there, glaring at each other. I think that the former, as he sat in that tree, confronted by the black rabble, must have hankered after the fleshpots of Egypt which he had left behind; he must have felt that liberty, after all, was not the sweet thing which it is said to be. Nevertheless, he showed a bold front to the black crew.

These, however, did not mean to let him escape. They were content to await developments. After a little, the cockatoo flew off; then there was a tremendous uproar among the crows, which, with one accord, gave chase. The clamour continued for some time, but I did not again see the cockatoo. The poor bird must eventually have been torn to pieces by the crows, unless he was rescued by his owner. Probably not one of those crows had previously set eyes on a cockatoo. They therefore could not have had any scores to pay off. They merely mobbed him because he was a strange, bizarre, living object, and their instinct teaches them to regard all such creatures as their enemies.

In Oudh, last cold weather, I put up a large owl out of a mango-tree. It was in the middle of the day and the crows were about. Two of them caught sight of the owl during his short flight to the next tree, and at once proceeded to mob him. They took up a position on each side of him, sitting as close to him as possible, so that he was literally wedged in between them. Neither crow, however, seemed inclined to commence the attack.

In a campaign of this kind, the words "masterly inactivity" may be said to sum up corvine tactics. The owl was not enjoying himself, for, in addition to having a "ribald crow" on each side of him, I was looking at him from below. He therefore took to flight. The crows gave chase, taking pecks at his back. I could not follow the rest of the hunt, since, as organs of progression, legs are no match for wings. Presently, however, the two crows returned to the *Bagh* and, judging by their cries of exultation, one at least of them must have secured a beakful of owl's feathers!

Here, again, the owl cannot be called an enemy of the crow. It is true that there is one species which is said to wring young crows' necks in the dead of night; but this owl did not belong to that species. The crows merely set upon the owl because it was a strange creature, and they regard all strange creatures as enemies, and mobbing is the treatment meted out by crows to their foes. Allied to this hostility to all strange-looking creatures is one of the most curious phenomena in nature—the brutal way in which a wounded animal is treated by its fellows. Instead of caring for it and tending it, they set upon it and kill it, being, apparently, quite indifferent to its cries.

The other day, while driving along the main street of Madras, I saw a crow whose legs had been tied to its tail. It looked a most ludicrous object as it ran along, and fully twenty crows were accompanying it, regarding it with hostile eyes. They probably eventually pecked it to death. I am told that there used to be a Madras Civil Servant who hated crows with a great hatred. It was his wont to catch these birds, shave off their feathers, and paint the bare skin red or blue. The birds thus disfigured were, on liberation, immediately set upon by their fellows and killed. "This habit," writes Lockwood Kipling, is "reported to have suggested a stratagem by which omnivorous gipsy folk catch crows. A live crow is spread-eagled on his back, with forked pegs holding down his pinions. He flutters and cries, and the other crows come to investigate his case and presently attack him. With claws and beak he seizes an assailant and holds him fast. The gipsy steps from hiding and secures and pinions the second crow. These two catch two more, the four catch four more, and so on, until there are enough for dinner, or to take into a town, where the crow-catcher stands before some respectable Hindu shop and threatens to kill the bird he has in his hand unless the Hindu pays for its liberation."

It is a well-known fact that cattle almost invariably attack and gore to death one of their companions which is in great distress. The case of the crows killing their shaven and painted companion is almost certainly to be explained by supposing that they mistake it for some strange bird. They mob it for the same reason that they mobbed the cockatoo.

It seems to me that the attacks of animals on their companions in sore distress may be accounted for in the same way. The crows, or the cattle, or whatever be the animal in question, do not recognize their companion on account of its strange antics; they take it for some enemy and attack it.

It may seem highly improbable that animals should make such mistakes. We must, however, bear in mind that the attacking animals are at the time so excited as to be almost beside themselves. The cries of a fellow in distress exert a most extraordinary effect on the species. The howls of a companion will often drive a dog almost mad.

I have sometimes been looking at a pariah dog, which for no apparent reason suddenly begins to howl. The other dogs of the village rush up excitedly, but, seeing no enemy, they begin to attack one another.

The howling of their companion has excited them so greatly that they have suddenly and momentarily lost their senses. So it may be with the cows or cattle when they attack a companion in distress. They rush up to the scene, maddened by the cries of their fellow, and see some object performing strange antics, so, without waiting to consider what they are doing, they attack it.

The naturalist, Hudson, looks upon this strange instinct which makes animals kill a companion in distress as the perversion, not of the instinct which teaches animals to mob all strange species, but of that which teaches gregarious creatures to go to the assistance of a companion attacked by some enemy. According to him, when the individuals of a family are excited to a sudden deadly rage by the cries of distress of one of their fellows, or by the sight of its bleeding wounds, or when they see it frantically struggling on the ground, or in the cleft of a tree or rock, as if in the clutches of a powerful enemy, they do not turn on it to kill it, but to rescue it. But there is no enemy to see, so they, in their blind rage, attack the one living thing present—the wounded friend in this case—in mistake for an enemy.

Whether the theory here put forward or that of Hudson meets with acceptance, it is obvious that this habit of attacking friends in distress is not wanton cruelty; it is a blunder of a useful instinct. It may seem shocking to us that animals are so ready to destroy life. We must, however, remember that the characters of animals are moulded by natural selection;

that in the animal kingdom there are no Ten Commandments. Among animals killing is no murder.

Natural selection, if allowed to work unchecked, produces a number of races which think only of themselves and their offspring; a fauna of Ishmaelites, of which the hand of every species is upraised against all others. This indiscriminate hostility is necessary in the interests of the species; it is exercised in self-protection, and not from wantonness. There is nothing Nero-like in the character of most animals. For the safety of the species it is necessary to consider every creature a foe until it has proved that it is not.

As young animals grow up, they are, so to speak, educated to distinguish at sight an enemy from a harmless species. But if a new creature appear, they have no experience to guide them, so rely upon their instinct, which teaches them that all unknown organisms are enemies. They therefore attack it and destroy it, if strong enough to do so. By acting in this way they are on the safe side. It may be a harmless creature, or merely a suffering member of their own species, but they do not stay to consider this. Delay may mean death, so they either flee from the strange object or set upon it and kill it.

THE SEVEN SISTERS

"The seven birds . . . that never part."

BABBLERS are the Bohemians of bird society. The Seven Sisters are to the rest of the fowls of India what the denizens of the Quartier Latin are to the remainder of Parisian Society. There is much to be said for an unconventional, restraint-free life. The poets, from Horace downwards, have hankered after such an existence.

It is, indeed, no small thing to be able to eat what one likes, drink what one likes, say what one likes, and do what one likes. Babblers enjoy all these advantages, and many more. Were there ever before, throughout all the geological ages, any birds so utterly indifferent to personal appearance? If a crow were to show himself in public in the unkempt condition of the average babbler, he would be forthwith socially ostracized; he would be blackballed by every corvine Club and never receive an invitation to dinner. Crows are great sticklers for etiquette, whereas babblers care not a fig for appearances.

"Liberté, Fraternité, Egalité" is the motto of these

birds, and they flourish under their republican constitution. There must be close upon a hundred species of babblers scattered over India. The family is an enormous one, and the most characteristic ornithological feature of the country. Go where you will in the "Land of Regrets," you will not be able to dodge the babblers. In every station, whether on the hills or plains, you will be confronted by companies of Seven Sisters.

In scarcely any two provinces will the same species greet you, but you will have no difficulty in recognizing each new form as a near relation of those you have already met. "I have often amused myself," says Jerdon, writing of the sisterhood, "in imagining that they are not inapt representatives of the Hindus; certainly as far as their frequent congregating together, and their incessant noisy chattering and gabbling, they agree; and were I disposed to carry on the similitude further, it would not, I think, be a difficult task. It is not a little remarkable, too, that in southern India there are several kinds which in some measure correspond in geographical distribution with the principal Hindu races of this part of the country."

What gives these birds so strong a family likeness is the slovenly appearance they all present. Babblers represent all the degrees of untidiness. First and foremost comes the *Crateropus canorus*, the common babbler of the plains of Upper India. This bird looks as though it were in imminent danger of falling to pieces; its tail appears to hang by a mere thread, and its wings droop as if they were broken.

THE BABBLER
(ONE OF THE SEVEN SISTERS)

It may be likened to the human being who refuses to recognize the use of a hair-brush, who persists in wearing *dirzie*-made clothes, although his friends warn him that he will one day be mistaken for a scarecrow, and who, as often as not, forgets to put on a necktie.

This babbler has, further, a voice which is a very fair imitation of the sound produced by a rusty axle in motion. Passing upwards, through a host of intermediate species, we come to another landmark, in the shape of *Malacocercus somervillei*, the common Bombay babbler, which, as "Eha" describes, "reminds you of old Jones who spends the day in his pyjamas." Eventually we ascend to the Madras babbler, *Malacocercus griseus*, which must be considered as the "toff" of the babbler brotherhood.

This bird is so well known, being found in numbers in every garden in South India, that all description is superfluous. No one but a blind man can help remarking the chattering greyish-brown birds with yellowish white heads which abound in Madras. The first ones I saw introduced themselves to me as I was driving out of the railway-station yard, three minutes after my arrival.

Some of these babblers are more hoary than others. I think that the older birds exhibit the whitest heads. The white on the head of the babbler fledgling is certainly not conspicuous. Babblers differ from all other birds in that the unit of the community is not the individual, nor even the family, but the Club.

Babbler society is made up of a number of little Clubs, each composed of from seven to a dozen members;

hence the popular name Seven Sisters, or Brothers, applied to the commoner forms. "The man in the street" has no word by means of which he can speak of a single member of the species. It is impossible to talk about "a seven sister." Nor is this defect in the popular vocabulary a serious one, for where, outside a museum, do you see a solitary babbler? Is it possible to think of one of these birds without a friend to which it can babble?

These little Clubs are not mere family affairs, for a babbler is a monogamist, and has at the most four children; and two and four make but six. Each little company of Seven Sisters is just an informal, free-and-easy, go-as-you-please Club, composed of members drawn together by identity of interest. Every babbler is greatly attached to its Club; even when bringing up a family the parents feed in company. The reason for this is not far to seek.

A babbler is a feeble little bird. Its beak is but a puny weapon, and its power of flight is so limited that it is probably unable to take an uninterrupted journey of a hundred yards. It is, therefore, obvious that, had the species not learned to profit by the homely proverb "union is strength," it would long ago have been swept off the face of the earth in the fierce struggle for existence. Thanks, however, to their clannishness, babblers are among the most widely distributed of birds in India.

It requires a very smart fowl to circumvent a party of Seven Sisters. Directly one of them espies an enemy it gives the cry of alarm. This is followed by a general excited twittering and screaming. Then the various members of the little company take cover, and remain silently in hiding until the danger is passed. Some babblers will unite and boldly beat off a bird which attacks them. The Madras ones are not so brave; they hold discretion to be the better part of valour.

So, for the sake of safety, the members of each little company keep together, hopping about and rummaging among fallen leaves for the minute insects upon which they feed.

The tiny community has no leader. All the members are equal. Any one may take the lead, and the rest seem to follow as a matter of course. As they saunter along together, the babblers keep up a constant flow of small talk. Their voices are not beautiful, and those not familiar with the birds are apt to mistake pleasant conversation for squabbling.

"Fighting?" says Phil Robinson, "not at all; do not be misled by the tone of voice. That heptachord clamour is not the expression of strong feelings. It is only a way they have."

Dick says: "Well, Bill, what luck?" "A bit of all right," replies Bill, with his mouth full. "Going strong, Jane?" asks Harry, as he discovers an insect on the under side of a decayed leaf. "What do *you* think?" squeaks Jane. "Old Bob's having a fine blow out!" remarks Tom, casually. Jack suddenly calls out: "My eye! here's a find," and then the whole Club rushes to see what he has found, each member chattering at the top of his voice.

It is wonderful how rare fights among babblers are.

A Club of human beings under such circumstances would not be half so amiable; there would be constant bickerings and squabbles. Cliques would be formed, which would soon terminate the existence of the Club.

Good fellows though babblers be, they have their enemies. The Brain-fever Bird, that wicked Indian cuckoo, selects the sisterhood as her victims. She places her egg among the beautiful glossy blue eggs of the Seven Sisters, and thus forces these to perform her nursemaid's work. But they do not seem to mind; they take things far too easily to be bothered by the strange appearance, voice, and habits of one of their nestlings. Nothing worries these birds. If one of them ever writes an autobiography he will certainly give his book the title "Hurrah for the life of a babbler!"

THE LIFE OF A SOLITARY WASP

OF all "the Tribes of my Frontier" none are more deserving of notice than the solitary wasp. Their ways are of even greater interest than those of the social hymenoptera, whose praises have been so admirably sung by Maeterlinck, Grant Allen, and others. Perhaps it is the lonely life led by the solitary wasps that gives them so much character; for character they certainly have. "So whimsical," writes Burroughs, "so fickle, so forgetful, so fussy, so wise, and yet so foolish, as these little people are; such victims of routine and yet so individual, such apparent foresight and yet such thoughtlessness, at such great pains to dig a hole and build a cell, and then at times sealing it up without storing it with food or laying the egg, half finishing hole after hole, and then abandoning them without any apparent reason; sometimes killing their spiders, at other times only paralysing them; one species digging its burrow before it captures its game, another catching its prey and then digging the hole; some of them hanging the spider up in the fork of a weed to keep it away from the ants while they work at the nest, and running to it every few minutes to see that it is safe; others laying the insect on the ground while they dig; one species walking backwards and dragging its spider after it, and when the spider is so small that it carries it in its mandible, it still walks backwards as if dragging it, when it would be much easier to walk forward. A curious little people, leading their solitary lives and greatly differentiated by their solitude, hardly any two alike, one nervous and excitable, another calm and unhurried; one careless in her work, another neat and thorough; this one suspicious, that one confiding; ammophila using a pebble to pack down the earth in her burrow, while another species uses the end of her abdomen—verily a queer little people, with a lot of wild nature about them, and a lot of human nature too."

A multitude of solitary wasps are found in Madras, many of which invade our houses and build their nests inside them. One of these, one of the Eumenidæ, recently forced herself upon my notice. She is known to entomologists as *Rhynchium brunneum*. She has no popular name. I use the pronoun "she" advisedly, for among wasps the male is an unimportant creature. He is smaller than the female, and takes no part in the construction or the provisioning of the nest.

The female of this particular wasp is about three-quarters of an inch long, her waist is short and thick, her body is brownish red in colour, marked posteriorly by three black bands which run across the body. Her glassy wings are of a brownish-yellow hue. Thus her garments are neither very beautiful nor very showy. She is clad in quiet, businesslike clothes which are quite in keeping with her calm, industrious habits.

A lady wasp of this species came, a little over a month ago, into a bedroom through an open window and began at once to look about her for a suitable site for her nest. Her attention was soon attracted by a wooden bed. In this she found some ideal nesting-places—the holes in the upright posts intended to receive the poles for mosquito curtains. Having elected to nest in these six-inch-deep cavities, the wasp promptly set to work to prepare them for her eggs.

She flew out of the window, to return in a few minutes, carrying between her front legs a pellet of mud, fully half the size of her body. She herself had prepared this pellet by means of her jaws and saliva out of dust collected on the roadside. She flew with it into the cavity, and proceeded to line it with mud. Having utilized her load, the industrious insect flew off and returned with a second load, and a third, and a fourth.

In a short time she had lined the hole, and the mud soon set as hard as mortar. I believe that directly the nest is lined the wasp lays an egg in it, but of this I cannot be sure, for it is impossible to see what is going on at the bottom of a hole six inches deep and less than an inch wide. It is therefore possible that the egg was laid at a later stage in the proceedings. The nest has now to be provisioned, for when the grub emerges from the egg in its underground cell it will need food. Accordingly the wasp mother goes forth to seek provender for her offspring upon which she will in all probability never set eyes. Consider for a moment the significance of this. We have, here, an insect toiling all day long for her offspring which she will never see. I do not think that she even knows that her eggs will give rise to young wasps. She toils for the benefit of these because that strange internal force which we call instinct compels her to do so. She knows not what she is doing, yet no human parent could work harder in the interests of her offspring. Analogy would lead us to think that the female wasp loves her children. Yet this is impossible. The question thus arises therefore in the case of the higher animals, how much of their solicitude for their offspring is due to affection and how much to blind instinct?

The grub which the egg will produce is both carnivorous and voracious, and, what is more, it must be fed upon fresh meat. Here, then, is a difficult problem which the wasp has to solve: how to provide fresh meat for her offspring. It is obviously useless to kill some creatures and place them underground, for by the time the young one hatches out the food will have become putrid. If, on the other hand, she catch some feeble creatures and put them alive into the nest, they will wriggle and struggle, so that, if they do not damage the egg, they will at least knock it away from them. This would be fatal were it to take place, for the grub, when it first emerges from the egg, is so weak that it cannot move by so much as a hair's breadth, so that it will starve to death unless it is hatched right in the midst of its food-supply.

Let us see how the wasp solves the problem. She presently returns carrying a thin greenish caterpillar quite as long as herself. She flies with it into the nest. She carries it lengthwise, grasping it with all her six legs. Having placed it in the cell, she flies out of the window and soon returns with another caterpillar of the same kind. When this is safely deposited in the nest she goes off for a third. Let us now take out and examine one of these caterpillars. It is apparently alive and unwounded, but, if alive, it is certainly completely paralysed, since it never makes the slightest motion. It is therefore evident that the wasp has done something to it. Has she killed it or merely paralysed it?

Leon Dufour, who first studied the ways of the hymenopteron *Cerceris*, which stores the nest with weevils, was of opinion that the wasp killed her prey and injected into it some antiseptic liquid to keep it fresh during the weeks or days her eggs took to hatch.

The great French entomologist Fabre, whose work, "Insect Life" (of which there is an English edition), every one should read, discovered that the antiseptic theory is incorrect and that the wasp only paralyses its prey. He proved conclusively that the wasp merely pricks the motor nerve centres of her victim and thus completely paralyses it. He actually saw a *Cerceris* wasp perform the operation. As she was returning with a paralysed weevil, Fabre snatched it away from her with pinchers, instantly throwing a living weevil in exchange. "The manœuvre," writes Fabre, "succeeded perfectly. As soon as the *Cercercis* felt the prey slip under her body and escape her, she stamped with impatience, turned round, and, perceiving the weevil which had replaced hers, flung itself upon it and clasped it in order to carry it away. But she promptly perceived that this prey was active, and then the drama began, and ended with inconceivable rapidity. The *Cerceris* faced her victim, seized its proboscis with her powerful jaws, and grasped it vigorously, and while the weevil reared itself up, pressed her forefeet hard on its back as if to force open some ventral articulation. Then the tail of the murderess slid under the *Cleonus*, curved and darted its poisoned lancet swiftly two or three times between the first and second pair of feet. In a twinkling all was over. Without one convulsive movement, with no motion of the limbs, such as accompany the death of an animal, the victim fell motionless for ever, as if annihilated.

"It was at once wonderful and terrible in its rapidity. Then the assassin turned the weevil on its back, placed herself body to body with it, her legs on either side of it, and flew off. Three times I renewed this experiment . . . the same scene always occurred."

In like manner does the wasp *Rhynchium*, of which we are speaking, paralyse her victim, with, however, one difference. There is in the weevil but one motor centre, so that the wasp has only to stab it in one place in order to completely paralyse it; a caterpillar, however, is a composite creature, having several motor centres; hence it has to be stabbed in three places before it is rendered quiescent—in the neck, in the hind part of the thorax, and in the abdomen. The first stroke gives the front part of the body its quietus, the second paralyses the front pro-legs, and the last stills for ever the movements of the hind pro-legs. The

wasp has a wonderful knowledge of the anatomy of caterpillars! "It is," writes Fabre, "in this triple blow that the infallibility, the infused science, of instinct, appear in all their magnificence."

These words are in the main true, but more recent investigations have shown that instinct is, in this case, not absolutely infallible. The wasp does sometimes make a "boss shot." It occasionally happens that a stab fails to reach the nerve ganglion. When the wasp has stored the cell with eight caterpillars she closes it by roofing it with mud. I believe that eight is the number of caterpillars she allows to each egg, but there again I speak not with certainty.

These observations were made at random and were often interrupted. After the cell had been closed there was still plenty of room left in the hole in the bed-post; in this space the wasp laid another egg, killed more caterpillars, and then closed the cell with mud, making the top of the roof flush with the summit of the post. She then proceeded to stock the hole in the bed-post, behaving in precisely the same way as before. Having completed the second nest, she forthwith began to line the third hole with mud, and was stocking it with caterpillars, when I cut short her life. I had to sacrifice her in the interests of science, in order to find out the species to which she belonged.

Five days after she had closed the first nest I opened it, and found that all the caterpillars had disappeared, and that a great fat white grub, fully an inch in length, had taken their place. This had emerged from the egg, and then devoured all the caterpillars. The length of time that the eggs require to hatch varies with different species, and is often considerably longer than the time occupied by the *Rhynchium* egg.

The larva soon passes into the pupal state. It does not spin a cocoon as the silkworm moth does. The transformation into the *imago* or adult occupies less than three weeks. As there is no cocoon, one might, if the creature could live in the light, watch the wonderful metamorphosis actually taking place, but light appears to kill the pupa. About seventeen days after the egg had been laid I dug out another pupa. It had assumed the adult wasp-like form, was almost white in colour, and looked what it was—an unfinished wasp.

Over the last cell I tied a piece of muslin to make a cage into which the imago would have to fly on leaving the nest, but I might have spared myself the trouble. Twenty-five days after the closing of the cell, I noticed that a hole had been gnawed in the muslin, and, looking into the nest, I saw a hole through the roof of the cell and knew that the wasp had flown. She had been able to adapt herself to circumstances. She had used her jaws, with which instinct had taught her to rasp away the roof of her cell, to cut a hole in the muslin, and thus gained her liberty.

PLAINTIVE CUCKOO (CUCOMANTIS PASSERINUS)

INDIAN CUCKOOS

IN the matter of cuckoos India can give points to the British Isles. The good folk at home see only one species of cuckoo, and that spends less than half its time on the British shores; we in India, on the other hand, can boast of an avifauna in which the sub-family *cuculinæ* is represented by no fewer than thirty species.

Lest the above statement should excite the righteous indignation of British ornithologists, let me hasten to say that it is not strictly true, that it requires a little modification.

Species of cuckoo, other than the common or garden *Cuculus canorus*, have been seen in England outside the Zoological Gardens. Three bold species have, at divers times, visited the shores of Albion, and warm was the reception each received.

Thanatology is a science carried to perfection in the Homeland. So-called naturalists shoot, at sight, every strange bird. In 1871 an American Black-Billed Cuckoo was seen at Belfast and shot. On five different occasions the Yellow-Billed Cuckoo—the American Rain-bird—has visited our shores only to be put to death. A similar fate overtook the two Great Spotted

Cuckoos that at different times ventured to set foot in the United Kingdom. Woe betide the strange bird who ventures near the hospitable shores of England! But let us leave this unpleasant subject. Let us turn to the Indian cuckoos, which are not persecuted by man.

The European cuckoo (*Cuculus canorus*) is a regular visitor to India. In the Himalayas during the months of April, May, and June its melodious voice is heard unceasingly from early morn to dewy eve. This bird does not venture in great numbers into the plains; but it does come, and has been seen as far south as the Godavery District.

The two essentially Indian cuckoos are our ubiquitous friends—the Brain-fever bird and the Koel. The former is known to scientists as *Hierococcyx varius*. It is also called the hawk-cuckoo, on account of its resemblance to a hawk. Its face is its fortune; for the little birds, when they see it, are said to mistake it for a hawk, and so allow it to drive them out of their nests and deposit its eggs in them. The "seven sisters" are its usual victims.

The brain-fever bird is, perhaps, the noisiest creature in India. It can boast of a variety of calls; the one of which it is most fond and which it utters throughout the hot weather, both by day and by night, is a penetrating *crescendo*, "brain fever, *brain fever*, BRAIN FEVER," which pierces one through and through. The koel (*Endynamys honorata*) is another vociferous cuckoo, which exhibits a great predilection for the climate of Madras. In that part of the world it is only less common than the crow. The male is a glossy black

THE KOEL, OR BLACK CUCKOO, FEMALE

bird, which, when seen during flight, looks like a slenderly built crow with an extra long tail. The female is a brown bird spotted with white. This species makes the crow do its nursemaid's work for it.

Needless to say, the Indian grey-necked crow is not the bird to be bluffed out of its nest by an ass in a lion's skin in the shape of a hawk-like cuckoo. If the hen-cuckoo went up threateningly to a crow and tried to enter the nest, the crow would probably remark, "Very sorry, ma'am, full inside, try outside!" It therefore becomes necessary for the koels to resort to artifice. The female, who is inconspicuously coloured, remains in the background, while the showy black cock bird swaggers up to the crow's nest upon which the pair have designs. As a rule, the mere sight of an adult male koel drives a crow almost mad with fury.

Nothing is commoner in India than the sight of a couple of crows chasing a koel. Indeed, the cuckoos are most unpopular with birds of all classes. They are the outlaws of the bird world; so they usually keep well to cover. When they do venture into the open they usually make a wild dash, like that of a boy from one "base" to another when playing at rounders.

Upon this occasion, however, the koel turns his unpopularity to account. If the sight of him is insufficient to provoke the crows at the nest to give chase, he begins to insult them. "Call that thing a nest?" he says mockingly. "Why, if I could not raise up a more respectable structure than that I would lay my eggs in some other bird's nest!" The crows, of course, will not tolerate this kind of thing. They give chase.

Now, in a race between a koel and a crow the latter has about as much chance of winning as a cart-horse would have if pittied against a Derby winner. The koel, however, is content to keep just ahead of his corvine pursuers; thus he lures them from the nest, and meanwhile his mate is placing her egg in it. When the male bird hears his wife's voice he knows that the fell deed is done, and so puts on a spurt and leaves his pursuers far behind, screaming as he disappears from view: "Get back to the nest, you blockheads, the eggs are getting cold!"

The crows realize that this is really their most sensible course. On their return they fail to recognize the prank which has been played upon them; and so hatch out the strange egg along with their own. But the curious thing is that when the young koel is hatched, its foster-parents do not wring its neck, but tend it most carefully.

Birds, when sitting on their eggs or looking after their young, are mere automatons, creatures of instinct. At this period they seem to cast intelligence to the wind, and to obey implicitly the promptings of instinct. Instinct teaches a bird to feed all the young in its nest without questioning their origin. We may thus account for the care which the crow parents lavish upon their koel foster-children.

But we have yet to overcome a further difficulty. How is it that when the young koels first begin to fend for themselves they are not set upon by the strange crows of the neighbourhood and devoured? A crow, as a rule, never loses an opportunity of attacking a

THE KOEL, OR BLACK CUCKOO, MALE

koel. Here would be a golden opportunity for them; they would experience no difficulty in catching or destroying a newly fledged cuckoo.

Some authorities have thought that during the earlier part of their life young koels retain the crow smell, and so are let alone by the strange crows they encounter. I do not think that this is the explanation.

Smell does not appear to play an important part in the life of a bird. Of all the avine senses that of smell seems to be the least well developed.

So far as my observation goes, it is the male koel which is chiefly attacked by the crows. I do not remember ever having seen a female chased; she is so different from the cock bird in appearance that it is possible that the crows do not know that she is a koel. Now young koels of both sexes resemble the female in plumage, and I think that it is to this fact that they owe their immunity from attack.

Cuckoos are, indeed, wonderful creatures. They are not content with victimizing poor helpless little birds; they select as their victims and dupes the boldest and bravest of the feathered race. The brain-fever bird victimizes the social and alert babblers. The koel chooses crows, of all birds.

Another cuckoo, the Drongo-cuckoo (*Surniculus lugubris*), goes one better. It selects as its dupe the valiant and ever-vigilant king-crow. As we have already seen, the king-crow is, during the nesting season, a little fury. It will attack any bird or beast that ventures near its nest. It takes no account of size. The cuckoo that desired to victimize it might be as big as the mythical roc; but this would profit the parasitic bird little: the king-crow would stand up to it. It is by craft, not by "bluff," that the cuckoo succeeds in "scoring off" the drongo. *Surniculus lugubris* is, perhaps, the most wonderful example of mimicry in nature. It has adopted the dress of the drongo. It is black all over and has a forked tail. It is said to be a very uncommon cuckoo.

I do not know whether I have ever seen a live species or not, for I cannot distinguish it from a king-crow. I am not ashamed of this admission: for the king-crow himself is in this respect no better off than I am. I submit that if A cannot distinguish B from his (A's) own brother, it is surely not to be expected that I, a stranger, can do so!

The drongo-cuckoo has a smart appearance and a straight flight, and thus differs from the majority of cuckoos, which are slovenly birds, the kind of birds which, if they wore clothes, would slouch about with their hands in their pockets and their hats on the back of the head. The drongo-cuckoo, the lion in the ass's skin, is allowed to hover about in the neighbourhood of a king-crow's nest, and seizes the opportunity of depositing an egg when the back of the owner of the nest is turned.

India boasts of some respectable cuckoos, that is to say, cuckoos which build nests and do not shirk parental responsibilities. The best known of these is that widely distributed bird, the coucal, or crow-pheasant. He is a personage of sufficient importance to demand a chapter to himself.

THE CROW-PHEASANT

THE deep, sonorous "*whoot, whoot, whoot*" of the crow-pheasant is one of the most familiar of the sounds which greet the rising sun in India. *Centropus sinensis*, although it is to be heard at all hours of the day, prefers to indulge in its vocal exercises in the early morning or at the sunset hour; hence its cry is often mistaken for that of some belated, or early-rising owl.

The crow-pheasant, however, is not an owl. With the exception of the voice, there is nothing owl-like about the bird. It is not a creature of the night. It is just a respectable cuckoo which brings up its own family. Needless to say, the other members of the cuckoo tribe disown it. It is not admitted to any of the cuculine clubs.

For the benefit of those who are not initiated into the mysteries of cuckoo society, I may say that the qualifications for admission to one of their clubs are, firstly, zygodactyle feet, and secondly, the making of the following solemn affirmation: "I bind myself never, under any circumstances whatsoever, to do myself that which it is possible to make others do for me." The coucal is able to satisfy the former of these conditions, but cannot honestly attach its signature to the affirmation.

The crow-pheasant is not a bird of great beauty. Nevertheless, I think that "Eha" is a little severe on it when he dubs it a great, awkward bird. I myself rather admire its shape, and should have nothing to say against the bird, did not its plumage not partake so much of the nature of patchwork. Its head, body, and tail are black, and its wings chestnut in hue. Black and brown do not form a happy combination. Why the birds of both sexes are thus attired I know not. This is one of the many unsolved problems of animal colouration.

Were the thing not impossible, one would think that at some beanfeast long ago the crow-pheasant must have imbibed a little too freely, and then, in a moment of maudlin friendship, exchanged wings with some brown bird. For the wings do not match the rest of the plumage, nor are they large enough for the bird, hence its decidedly laboured flight. The smallness of its wings, however, does not worry the coucal, for it does not use those appendages much. It lives in thick cover, although it often ventures out in the open to feed. When alarmed, it flaps up to the nearest tree and then disappears from view in a mysterious way. As a tree-climber there is no other bird of the size which can approach a crow-pheasant.

It is most amusing to watch him seeking his breakfast, which consists chiefly of insects. The bird picks his food off the ground and hunts by preference in the neighbourhood of water. His walk is best described as a "mincing gait." He evidently does not mean to trip, for he lifts his feet absurdly high at each step. He never hops; he would not do anything so vulgar.

The manner in which he picks up his food is in accordance with his gait. He does not, like the hoopoe or the common or garden fowl, greedily gobble up everything he comes across. He picks and chooses. He gives one the idea that he is an epicure. Whether this is so or not, he undoubtedly feeds with great caution.

His whole attitude is that of looking before he leaps. He goes systematically along a hedge, casting, as he progresses, frequent glances to right and left, occasionally pulling something small out of the ground—presumably a grub or an insect. Now and again, he will penetrate the hedge, for, like small boys, he is addicted to worming his way into dense thickets merely for the fun of the thing.

Having eaten up everything to his taste in the vicinity of the hedge, the crow-pheasant will take to the open, progressing with the same mincing steps and looking about with the utmost wariness, and if he perceives a human being, he will at once make for the nearest tree. If the coast seems clear, the bird continues his stately progress. Suddenly he espies a grasshopper. He then casts off his phlegmatic air and makes a most undignified dash at the insect. The latter is usually too quick for him, and hops off, but the crow-pheasant is not to be denied; he jumps after it, being assisted by his wings.

An exciting chase usually ensues, in which it is not

safe for the sportsman to lay his money on either the little insect or the great fowl. The grasshopper often doubles, and is of course followed by the coucal, which, when making a sharp turn, often expands one wing, using it as a steering apparatus. The bird is said also to eat lizards and snakes. He possibly eats small frogs, for I have often seen crow-pheasants wading in water.

The nest is an interesting object. It is usually situated in the midst of some impenetrable thicket, for a coucal dislikes having his family affairs pryed into. It is a great structure, about the size of a football, composed chiefly of sticks. It is roofed in and has the entrance at the side. In spite of its size, it is usually so well concealed that it is not an easy thing to discover. Sometimes, when one knows for certain that there is a nest in a thicket, it is impossible to find that nest without pulling down the greater part of the bush round about it. I once spent a couple of hours looking in vain for a nest which I knew to be in a thick hedge; then I told off two peons to find it without doing any damage to the hedge. They professed their inability to discover it, but I do not believe they made very sustained efforts to find it; I rather fancy they regarded the duty as beneath the dignity of their position! Whether this was so or not, it is certain that the crow-pheasant is an adept at concealing his home.

The coucal is usually described in works on natural history as a shy bird. It is certainly exceedingly shy in Madras, much more so than it is in Northern India. The reason of this difference in behaviour is not apparent, for besides the innocent "griff" who shoots the bird in mistake for a pheasant, the lower caste Hindu folk of all parts of India, and most Mohammedans, look upon the flesh of the bird as a great delicacy. Hence the coucal is frequently trapped.

Yet the bird in Northern India is comparatively tame. In Madras, too, it is trapped; there are usually two or three wretched-looking crow-pheasants to be seen in the Moore Market. These are kept in cages so small that their tails are crushed up against the wires, and the poor birds look the picture of misery, and are doubtless as unhappy as they look.

Even worse is the plight of the king-crows which are caught and kept in cages. These birds are, presumably, not eaten, and I do not think they are kept as pets, for so lively a bird as a king-crow could not live long in a cage. They are, presumably, caught and ill-treated merely to induce kind-hearted folk to pay for their liberation.

This is commonly done with crows. These birds are trapped and then taken to a Brahmin by some disreputable character, who threatens to destroy them, then and there, unless the Brahmin pays for the bird's liberation. It is surely time that these practices should be made punishable by law.

A STUDY IN ANIMAL CHARACTER

A WELL-KNOWN naturalist declares that "among animals there is not the same diversity of individual character as among men, nor the same variety; all the individuals of one species are cast pretty much in the same simple mould." It is true that the character of birds and beasts is less complex than that of human beings; nevertheless, among the higher animals there is sufficient complexity of character to allow of very great variation. So far from animals of the same species being cast in the same mould, they often exhibit very marked differences in manners, habits, temperament, and tastes. Just as no two creatures are alike in bodily form, so do no twain exactly resemble one another in temperament.

A stroll in the garden will furnish evidence of this. You come upon a company of "seven sisters" rummaging among dried leaves and picking up unconsidered trifles. The birds are, of course, keeping up a running conversation. Babblers, like Madrassi coolies, can do nothing without singing and shouting. One of the little company catches sight of you and informs his friends of your presence. The more timid of the brotherhood immediately fly off. The rest remain eyeing you suspiciously, and wondering what they shall do. Presently the fright of those which have already betaken themselves to cover communicates itself to some of the birds which have maintained their ground. Such fly to shelter. You approach nearer. This is the signal for others to take to their wings, and perhaps all have left, except one sturdy fellow, who looks at you in such a way that he seems to say: "I'll be blowed if I move until I am obliged to."

Here, then, we have in this little company of six or seven a number of types of character, ranging from excessive timidity to great temerity. The "seven sisters" do not form an isolated case. Almost every company of birds exhibits a similar phenomenon. We know so little of Nature's wild creatures that our books contain no accounts of these distinctions in character. Naturalists are content to describe the typical member of each species; they omit to mention the thousand and one variations from it.

This, doubtless, accounts for the origin of the idea that all animals of a species are cast in the same mould. To take an example, the Indian crow is described as a bold, bad bird, which leads a depraved life of aimless vagabondage. This is doubtless a true description of the typical crow. But there are degrees of wickedness, even among crows. It is possible that some of the *corvi* lead useful and admirable lives. For aught I know, there may be crow philanthropists, crows which spend their life slumming, holding tea-parties, delivering lectures, and doing other good works.

GREEN SHANK (ONE OF THE KUCH NÉS OF THE INDIAN SHIKARI)

We catch but fleeting glimpses of wild animals; hence it is not easy to study their idiosyncrasies. Fortunately, there are the domestic animals. These come to our help. Every horse, cat, dog, cow, and fowl has its own little character, which is displayed in its actions. It is to these creatures that we must turn if we should study character among animals.

Two fox-terriers allow me to share the bungalow with them, so that I have an excellent opportunity of observing their idiosyncrasies. They are what the Babu would call he-dogs, and rejoice in the respective names of *Tony* and *Bob*. So great is the diversity of character which they exhibit that, after watching them for a few weeks, one feels capable of writing a canine "Sandford and Merton."

The lineage of neither of these dogs is unimpeachable. There are bars sinister on the escutcheon of each. *Bob* is a stolid, squarely built animal, exhibiting distinct traces of the bull-terrier. He reminds one of a Dutch burgher; he is eminently respectable, although not of prepossessing appearance. *Tony* is a lanky dog, a canine "daddy-long-legs." He has been allowed to run to seed and has developed into a fragile weed of a hound. He has a pretty face, but his beauty is not patrician; it is, in fact, distinctly plebeian, being that of a glorified pariah dog. His worst enemies could not call him phlegmatic, but they might hint that he is afflicted with St. Vitus's dance.

Bob's character is in keeping with his appearance. There is in it much of sterling merit. He is an austere dog, despising the vain pomp and glory of this world.

He knows what obedience is, although he sometimes acts as if he did not. He is slow to make friends among men, but once made he retains them by faithful devotion. He is not demonstrative in his friendship. He has been known to wag his tail; but he performs this action sedately and decorously, I might say, half-heartedly. He never dreams of wagging the whole posterior end of his body, as some dogs do. He is enthusiastic over nothing, not even his food. You hand him a bone; he accepts it with a *blasé* indifference which is quite refreshing. He has no pretty, winning ways, no mischievous tricks. He is essentially a man's dog.

Tony is what the women-folk call an "affectionate dog"—this means that he makes friends with every stranger who comes within the gates. The more strange the person, the more pleased is *Tony* to see him. He is fond of all men, and loves eatables as himself. He is as partial to the kitchen as a schoolboy to the tuck shop. Mischievous, restless, and disobedient, *Tony* is the canine counterpart of the bad boy whose diary we all read with delight.

Bob, although, unlike the volatile *Tony*, he does not spend his days in cutting mad capers, in trying to catch his own tail and committing other such frivolities, likes exercise in moderation. He is distinctly fond of *shikar*, and is quite content to sit half the day under a tree contemplating with eager eyes the squirrels, which are disporting themselves among the branches and openly insulting him. At night, when the squirrels are asleep in their dreys, the musk-rats give him sufficient exercise to keep his body in health.

THE NIGHT HERON

Tony spends his days in running about like the proverbial March hare. Except when asleep, he is never still. He is not a good sporting dog. His idea of *shikar* is to chase an aged, inoffensive rooster, or to bait some unfortunate tethered calf.

Bob leads a sober and orderly life. I have never seen him looking dishevelled. *Tony*, on the other hand, reminds one of the inky-fingered, dirty-collared, tieless urchin, who habitually plays truant. He cannot enjoy a run in the garden without discovering a dirty puddle. This, in his opinion, requires investigation.

Tony, by the by, investigates everything; he has an inquiring mind. The invariable result of his investigation is that the dirtiest portions of that puddle find themselves transferred to the person of *Tony*. They are borne off triumphantly, clinging to his paws and body. *Tony* then proceeds to make the grand tour of the house, leaving behind him footprints, not on the sands of time, but, what comes to much the same thing, on the drawing-room carpet. When thus bespattered with mud, *Tony* is always more demonstrative than usual. He jumps up at each of his human friends in turn, and, heedless of their remonstrances, proceeds to make their garments as muddy as his own feet.

Bob has not many dog friends. He is naturally reserved; he makes no advances to his neighbours. His solemn face, muscular frame, and powerful teeth prevent these from forcing themselves upon him. *Tony* is "hail-fellow, well met" with every *Dick*, *Tom*, and *Harry* of a pariah dog. He draws the line at nothing. No animal is too disreputable-looking, too mangy, too much of a cur to be *Tony's* friend. The result of this cosmopolitanism is that he and all the bazaar dogs of the neighbourhood are as "thick as thieves." *Tony* hates *Bob* with a mighty hatred, and *Bob* loathes *Tony* with a great loathing. The consequence is that when the heroes meet there is much growling and gnashing of teeth. For this reason they are not allowed to see much of each other. It is hoped that they will one day settle down to a kind of armed neutrality.

PADDY-BIRDS AND EGRETS

THE paddy-bird, *alias* the pond heron, *alias* the blind heron, *alias Aideola grayii*, is one of the few animals that really understand the art of loafing. Unlike the majority of the feathered tribe, he makes no pretence of being busy. He does nothing all day, and does not try to hush up the fact. Nor does he endeavour to delude himself into believing that the day is not long enough for the work he has to get through. The paddy-bird lives chiefly on frogs.

I do not know the extent of the appetite of a pond heron, never having had to cater for one. Nevertheless, were I given the contract to feed a number of them, I would not allow more than three frogs per head *per diem.* If any bird clamoured for more, I would promptly set him down as a glutton, and make him mortify the flesh by fasting once a week.

Now, to a professional fisherman, the capture of three frogs per day is not an Herculean task, yet this constitutes the average daily labour of a paddy-bird; it is not sufficient to debar the bird from belonging to a trade union. I am of opinion that every pond heron, when about to die, might say with truth, " I have never done an honest day's work in my life!" He stands all day, presumably because he is too lazy to sit, looking as though he were thinking of his grandmother, or posing for his photograph. He does not often condescend to seek his prey. He prefers to wait for the food to come to him, which it seems to do with unfailing regularity. The bird is a philosopher, his philosophy being of the description enunciated in the well-known song entitled "You've got to have 'em, whether you want 'em or not" (the "'em" in this case denoting mothers-in-law, measles, etc.). Although he does not strictly follow the advice to open his mouth and shut his eyes and see what somebody sends him—for it is utopian, impossible of attainment—he does what in the end comes to much the same thing. He stands with his mouth shut and eyes open until a juicy frog passes his way, when he seizes and swallows it.

Up-country the paddy-bird is so absurdly tame as to receive the name of "blind heron." Those that dwell in Madras are far more wary. I suspect that they are highly esteemed as table-birds by the unsophisticated Madrassi; hence the unusual shyness.

The paddy-bird flies as little as possible. He takes the minimum amount of exercise necessary to keep himself in good health, just sufficient, indeed, to stave off attacks of liver. During most of the day he takes up his position in some puddle, where he stands motionless for hours, by preference in a strange attitude. He would make a perfect artist's model. If he could only look pleasant he would be a subject after the heart of the photographer. But so sad a bird is he that I fear

PADDY BIRD

the exhortation, "Think of 'er," would scarcely raise a smile from him.

As he stands and contemplates his image in the murky waters of the village pond, he forms a strange contrast to *dhobis*—the other denizens of the tank—who seem to work with might and main, the livelong day, trying to dash garments to pieces against a rugged stone, under the impression that they are doing a little washing. The look of silent contempt which the paddy-bird bestows on the perspiring, grunting washerman would make the latter feel very uncomfortable if he only had the leisure to notice it. The *dhobi* and the paddy-bird form perfect contrasts; yet they have one common feature. They are both anomalies. The washerman is the exception which proves the rule that Orientals are placid individuals who never do a stroke of unnecessary work. The blind heron is the exception which proves the rule that birds are active, busy, bustling creatures.

The paddy-bird, to adapt one of Mr. Phil Robinson's happiest phrases, sits all dingy gray and flies all white. As he loafs on the margin of the murky water he is an inconspicuous object. His brownish plumage, dirty yellow beak, and dingy green legs are all of the hue of the environment. As he takes to his wings the bird is transfigured. He is changed, as if by fairy touch, into a beautiful milk-white bird. His pinions are large, their under surface is snow-like, and they are so conspicuous as he floats through the air that they distract the eye from all else. The human eye is able to obtain only a general impression of a moving object. A flying kingfisher is a flash of light blue, and a redstart one of fiery red. The most conspicuous feature of the moving thing seems, as it were, to obliterate, to render invisible, all others.

Thus, when horses are racing, the attitude which is so striking as to swallow up all others is that of the straining animals with extended legs. As a matter of actual fact, the horses' legs are doubled up under the body just as frequently as they are stretched out. The doubled-up horse is, however, not a striking object, so the eye fails to retain it, and notices only the panting steeds with outstretched legs. This phenomenon accounts for the fact that photographs of racing horses are almost always disappointing; they appear unnatural and seem to exhibit the animals in all manner of impossible and awkward attitudes.

During flight the paddy-bird emits at intervals a guttural croak—not a cheerful sound, but one in keeping with the character of the bird. When at rest his appearance is not prepossessing. His attitude is misanthropic. He looks as though he shunned the company of other birds, and desired above all to be allowed to remain in peace. Yet the paddy-bird is not a quarrelsome creature. Dozens will sit in a row along the margin of a lake, separated by short intervals, and not one will take the least notice of any of the others. I have never seen two paddy-birds fighting. I have, indeed, seen one fly up to where another was standing, but the latter promptly flew away, without even casting a backward glance at the intruder. The truth is that it requires two energetic persons to organize a fight, and where are these to be found in paddy-bird society?

THE NIGHT HERON

At the advent of the monsoon, when the frogs begin to croak in deafening chorus, the male birds "go a-courting." They assume nuptial ornaments which consist of a ruff and some maroon feathers. The hen birds deck themselves out in similar finery, which is very annoying of them, for they thus present to naturalists a very awkward problem. Neither natural nor sexual selection will explain this change in both sexes. The dingy brown hue cannot be improved upon so far as the former is concerned, and, if this be doffed in deference to sexual selection—the preference of the ladies for bright colours—how are we to account for the change in the female? It would rather seem that the change is an adventitious one, connected with the reproductive function, and not in any way benefiting the bird.

It is scarcely necessary to state that the paddy-bird's nest, which is built in a tree, is an untidy structure, made of sticks, and is, in every way, in keeping with the general character of the bird.

The cattle egret (*Bubulcus coromandus*) is nearly related to the paddy-bird.

Never did two kinsmen present a greater contrast. The pond heron is solitary, inconspicuously coloured, and sluggish even for a heron. The cattle egret is gregarious, conspicuously clothed in white, and is the most energetic member of the heron tribe. It does not wait for its food to come to it, but "walks up" the insects upon which it feeds. It not infrequently makes a cow act as its beater.

Insects, whatever Lord Avebury may say to the

contrary, are not intelligent creatures. They seem to lead a blissful, happy-go-lucky life. They refuse to be worried; they decline to be always on the *qui vive* watching for the devourer who may never come their way. If they are caught, well—they are caught. That is the long and the short of it. It is true that Nature has given many of them clothes calculated to render them as inconspicuous as possible, but most of the insects seem unable to understand how to profit by their disguises. It is useless to dress up an ass to look like a lion, if the animal will persist in braying upon every possible occasion.

Whenever there is a commotion in the grass the grasshoppers and their friends jump into the air and thus show themselves to their enemies; whereas, had they the common sense to lie low, they might not be detected. Of course there is the point of view of the insect. I can quite imagine one turning round and saying: "It is all very fine for you to talk of sitting still in presence of danger. Try it yourself. If you were seated in your garden quietly taking afternoon tea and you saw a great monster, as big as the Albert Hall, coming towards you and making the earth shake as if it were in the throes of an earthquake, I am prepared to bet you two to one in antennæ that you would take to your heels and run for your life!"

Well, perhaps, there is after all something to be said for the insects, but the stern fact remains that, when surprised by a cow, they jump out of the way of its feet and find they have leapt out of the frying-pan into the fire, for, before they realize what has happened,

CATTLE EGRETS

they find themselves being roughly hustled down what they take to be a dark cavern, but which is, in reality, the gullet of a myna or an egret. These birds look upon cattle as organisms created solely to act as beaters for them. It is, therefore, quite evident that there is no need for an egret to be inconspicuously coloured in order to obtain its meals. It may dress as it pleases. It affects white except when it goes a-courting, when it arrays itself in gorgeous plumes and is then as proud as 'Arriet when she issues forth resplendent in her Sunday finery.

The difference in the food consumed accounts for the difference between the two species in habits and appearance.

When I want to shoot a black buck I don inconspicuous clothing and go forth alone into the jungle and stealthily stalk my game. But if I am after quail or snipe I take no pains to render myself inconspicuous. I like friends to accompany me and employ beaters to put up the birds. In the former case I hunt *à la* paddy-bird, in the latter I do a little *shikar* after the manner of the cattle egret.

ALEXANDER THE COPPERSMITH

ALL Anglo-Indians are acquainted with the voice of the coppersmith bird, although, possibly, some do not know him by sight. His unceasing, monotonous, metallic *Tonk, tonk, tonk* is perhaps the most striking of all the familiar sounds of an Indian garden. It is this which has given him his popular name. His note bears a remarkable resemblance to the sound of a hammer tapping upon metal. And, as the human coppersmith in the gorgeous East seems to spend most of his day in aimlessly hammering copper, it is easy to trace the origin of the bird's name. Indeed, the resemblance has struck both Indians and Europeans.

The notes of different individuals of the species are often of a different pitch. Some call more rapidly than others: when therefore two neighbouring birds sing simultaneously they give rise to the phenomenon of musical beats. The note of the coppersmith is by no means unpleasant; nevertheless, in this, as in all other cases, familiarity breeds contempt, and most Anglo-Indians are of opinion that they hear too much of the bird, and agree with Lockwood Kipling that "when you are down with fever and headache, you wish the noisy bird would take a holiday or go on strike."

Since the coppersmith's note is not confined to the breeding season, it is presumably not a love song designed to attract the attention of the opposite sex. Further, every bird seems to be able to emit but one note, and, as it will pour this forth by the hour at times when apparently there is not another member of the species within earshot, the note cannot be conversational.

I believe that the song of most birds is simply an ebullition of surplus energy, an expression of perfect health, an outward and audible token of pure and unalloyed happiness. I do not mean to say that birds cannot communicate vocally with one another, for they can and do. Their calls are, however, sharp, short notes, easily distinguishable from their songs.

Just as a man, when he is in good health and spirits, will sing while having his bath, so do the little coppersmiths pour forth their notes. In the former case, the pleasing contact of the water braces the nerves and forms the immediate stimulus; in the latter, it is sunshine that sets the birds' vocal cords in motion.

Coppersmiths love not the cold; consequently they do not ascend the hills. In Northern India, during the cold weather, their voice is completely hushed; but as soon as the warmer days come, the birds strike up; and, the hotter the weather, the more vociferous they grow. Thus the coppersmith bird might be called nature's thermometer. It will not, as a rule, sing if the temperature falls below 70°, while the warmer the weather, the louder is its note. In Madras the thermometer is rarely in the sixties; hence all day and every day we hear the coppersmith "toiling at his green forge."

The fact that the bird will not sing when the weather is cold bears out the theory that its note is merely an expression of happiness. When the temperature is low the coppersmith is miserable, so refuses to sing. Nature may be cruel in many respects. She is undoubtedly a hard task-mistress, for she ruthlessly destroys all the unfit. She is not a philanthropist; she provides her children with neither hospitals nor almshouses, for she has no halt or maimed or blind to look after. Her creatures perish the moment they become weakened by disease. Is this cruelty, or is it the truest kindness? Is it better to prolong a sick animal's misery, or to destroy the suffering creature?

The drastic procedure of Dame Nature is certainly fraught with good results. All her creatures enjoy perfect health, health such as is vouchsafed to few civilized men. Birds and beasts in their natural state are therefore perfectly happy, and the songs which fill the welkin are the expression of this happiness.

The coppersmith is not a difficult bird to see; he is not of a retiring disposition, nor does he attempt to avoid publicity. He likes to sit upon the topmost bough of a lofty tree; as often as not he selects a branch devoid of leaves, and there pours forth his eternal *Tonk, tonk, tonk,* wagging his head from side to side by way of beating time. The result of this head-wagging is that the bird's note seems to come from a direction other than it really does, and, on this account, it is difficult to "spot" the bird, in spite of its loud note and conspicuous perch.

Ornithologists have saddled this bird with the name of *Xantholæma hæmatocephala.* Since many persons will find this rather a mouthful, it is necessary to remark that it is scientifically correct to call the bird the crimson-breasted barbet. He is a coarse, showy bird. He may often be seen in the Moore Market at Madras, and, not infrequently, hawkers in the Mount Road offer the bird for sale. There are usually some coppersmiths in the Museum, in a cage near the entrance. These birds are made to share a dwelling with other species, such as Brahminy mynas. Under such conditions the coppersmiths never survive long. It is not that they are killed by the other inmates of the cage or that they cannot endure confinement. The reason of their speedy death is that the grain which is meat to so many birds is death to the coppersmith. If the latter be fed purely on fruit, he will often survive long in captivity. But the captive bird is not happy; no matter how warm the weather be, he never goes to work at his forge.

But this is a digression. To return to the appearance of the bird. It always puts me in mind of a woman who "makes up" very carelessly, who is not only exceedingly lavish of the paint, but does not understand how to shade it off gradually. The general colour of the bird's plumage is greenish, but on close inspection many greyish-white feathers are seen to be mingled with the green ones. There is a daub of crimson on the forehead and another on the throat. The sides of the face are pale yellow. The legs are coral-red. The build of the bird is exceedingly coarse.

COPPERSMITH

The sparrow, when seen side by side with the coppersmith, looks almost a gentleman! The coppersmith is the coarsest bird of my acquaintance, with the exception of the vulture. The coarseness of this latter, however, is of a different type; it is that of the despised outcast, while that of the coppersmith is the coarseness of a Whitechapel prize-fighter.

The coppersmith belongs to the barbet family. This is represented in India by seventeen species. The whole clan resemble one another very closely in habits. All live almost entirely on fruit. All have a loud, monotonous note. All are essentially tree-hunting birds. I do not remember ever having seen a barbet sitting on the ground. All nest in holes in trees.

The flight of every member of the family is undulating. The barbets are thus what men of science call a well-marked natural family. When you have once seen one, you cannot mistake its relations, nor confuse them with any other birds. The woodpeckers are perhaps their nearest relatives.

Coppersmiths nest only once in the year, about March in most parts of India, but earlier in Madras. The bird excavates a hole in a tree in much the same way as a woodpecker does. The coppersmith's beak, however, is not so efficient a pick-axe as that of its more highly specialized cousin. For this reason barbets usually select a place in a tree where the ants have been at work, and the wood is, in consequence, beginning to decay. When once the site has been decided upon, the excavation of the nest does not take long. A couple of days usually suffice.

The birds, both male and female, work like Trojans, and in this respect set a good example to human workmen. The husband and wife labour at the nest in turn. Each relief lasts about a quarter of an hour. The nest has no lining of any kind; the eggs are laid on the bare wood, and the young, when hatched, have to lie on this hard couch. It has never been my good fortune to follow closely the nesting operations of the coppersmith. However, a pair of green barbets (*Thereiceryx zeylonicus*) once nested in an old *pipal* tree in my garden compound at Fyzabad, and so afforded me an opportunity of noting some of their habits.

Although the green barbet is found in most parts of India, he is not so well known as his cousin, the coppersmith. His cry is a loud *Kurtur, kurtur, kurturuk.* He would be a handsome bird but for his face. This is not sarcasm. Among birds the face is not so vital a feature as with human beings. A fine figure and beautiful feathers, rather than good features, determine whether a bird is handsome or otherwise. The plumage of the green barbet leaves little to be desired. Essentially a bird of the greenwood tree, it partakes of the hue of its surroundings. As it flies among the branches its plumage appears to be of a uniform rich leafy green—the colour of the foliage in England after a rainy July day. Some brown feathers are visible in the head and neck, giving them a golden sheen under the influence of the sun's rays.

The bird has, however, a bare patch of yellow skin round each eye, which gives it a worn, haggard appearance, and greatly detracts from its beauty. Jerdon states that these naked patches are inflated when the bird emits its note. I have not been able to verify this, for the bird, when it pours forth its monotonous song, likes to conceal itself in tall, leafy trees.

To return to the nest in my compound. It was excavated in a bare branch of a *pipal* tree (*Ficus religiosa*) about ten feet above the level of the ground. The entrance to the nest pointed upwards, but was so well shaded by the foliage above that it was not flooded by some heavy rain that fell before the young birds were fledged.

Upon one occasion I watched the mother leave the nest, and then took up a position immediately under it, in order to ascertain whether she would venture in with me so near at hand. In a few minutes she returned, but, seeing me, alighted on a branch above that containing the young birds. There she sat and contemplated me. She next flew to a neighbouring branch, then back again. After thus behaving for about three minutes she summoned up her courage and flew into the nest. I could almost have touched her as she did this, so close was I. She made no pretence of concealing the whereabouts of the nursery, for, not only did she enter it before my eyes, but as soon as she was inside, she and the youngsters began talking loudly. In this case maternal anxiety seems to have got the better of prudence. On another occasion I saw a parent bird enter the nest with something in its beak. I wanted to have a good look at it as it emerged, so ran up close to the nest, but, as I did so, trod on some dried leaves, and the bird took alarm and flew out again without having fed her children. She went to the next tree and there stood and looked at me with a very large berry in her beak; she remained for some time in that attitude, and then, herself, swallowed the fruit. Judging from the efforts she made in disposing of it, the berry must have been an exceedingly hard one, and I take credit to myself for saving a young barbet from a violent attack of indigestion!

Barbets, like most birds, are very unwilling that any animal should approach their nest. One afternoon a myna chanced to perch upon the bough in which the above-mentioned nest had been excavated. Immediately afterwards one of the parent barbets happened to return. Without a second's hesitation it flew at the astonished myna, who had no idea of the existence of the barbet's nest. The myna hopped with great speed on to the next branch, and there stood looking at the barbet, and his attitude expressed mingled surprise and pain caused by the thought that any bird could behave so rudely to him. The barbet again "went for" him, and the myna, mystified, but thinking discretion the better part of valour, flew away. And he did well, for a myna is no match for a barbet. Indeed, if we may believe Layard, this latter is an exceptionally fierce bird. He states that a barbet kept in captivity used to devour its fellow-prisoners, who were inoffensive munias.

I hoped to witness the first attempt at flight of the young barbets, but was doomed to disappointment, for, being "by thronging duties press'd," the time I was able to devote to the young barbets was limited. I, however, saw indications that the time was at hand when the youngsters would trust themselves to the air, for their voices became more powerful, and the visits of the parent birds to the nest grew less frequent. As they began to wax strong, the youngsters would take it in turn to look out of the window of the nest and contemplate, with awe-struck eyes, the wondrous world.

At first they did not fear me, but would watch me with great curiosity; after a few days, however, curiosity gave way to fear, the birds seemed to learn that man was an enemy to be shunned, for they would disappear as soon as I approached the nest. One day I passed by and saw no little bird looking out, nor did any sound come from the nest. In vain did I wait to hear the well-known cry. Then I realized that the young barbets had begun in earnest to fight the battle of life.

Barbets are said to nest in the same hole year after year. It is not easy to prove this assertion; indeed, the only way of doing so would be for some person who has a fixed abode in India to catch a bird whose nesting place was known and to tie a piece of cotton to its leg, or give it some other recognition mark, and then wait and see whether it nested in the same hole next year. Jerdon states that the same nest is repeatedly used, and that each year fresh excavations take place, so that the original cottage in which the whole family once pigged must in course of time develop into what a house-agent would call a "palatial mansion."

So closely do the habits of the coppersmith resemble those of the green barbet, that the above account of the nesting operation might apply equally well to either species. In the Madras Museum there is an exhibit of a coppersmith's nest which was cut in a casuarina tree. The exhibit shows a young hopeful, looking out of the nest, with a wide-open beak, its invariable attitude when it catches sight of its parents. In nature, young birds do not, I think, as a rule, put their heads so far out of the nest, but the fact that the bird in the Museum does so has the advantage of enabling one to see that in plumage it differs from the adult in the absence of the crimson patches on the head and breast!

THE SPOTTED OWLET

PLINY describes the owl as the "very monster of the night." The Indian spotted owlet (*Athene brama*) goes one better than Pliny's bird, for, in addition to being the very monster of the night, it is the terror of the early and the closing hours of the day. This amusing little creature is the characteristic night bird of India. Just as the Indian day would be unthinkable without the crows, so would the night not seem itself were there no spotted owlets to disturb our slumbers.

When I first came to the "gorgeous East" I was sent, presumably by way of introduction to the rigours of the climate of this delightful country, to a station on the borders of the Punjab desert. Life in a desert is not without its advantages. For example, mosquitoes are conspicuous by their absence. There are some climates at which even the anopheles draws the line. During the winter months I had not much to complain of, save that the surrounding country was brown instead of green. The place was merely Aden without the sea and the rocks. By the middle of March the bungalow was an oven, hence beds were placed outside. In our compound was a great banyan tree, which was the concert hall of some spotted owlets.

I noticed that Colonel Cunningham states that the spotted owlet is noisy only at nightfall and dawn. "During the course of the night," he writes, "they are usually very silent." This statement is doubtless true of the Calcutta owlets, which are possibly somewhat subdued and overawed by the vice-regal presence. The spotted owlet of the United Provinces is not thus kept in order, it behaves most riotously the whole night. I do not go so far as to assert that the histrionic performances of every bird continue unceasingly throughout the night; all I say is that the incantations never cease. If it is not one bird that originates them, then it is another.

The goings-on of this owlet in Northern India are thus described by Mr. W. Jesse: "It keeps up a succession of street fights; and its squabblings and screechings are worse than a whole parish of cats collected in one back area." The owls in our banyan tree became such a nuisance that a court was held, and the birds were condemned to death. One holiday was devoted to an archery meeting. The result of this was that the whole family of jungle owlets suddenly departed unto their fathers. We, like the murderer of poor cock robin, had killed them with our bow and arrow. After that, our nights were comparatively peaceful. Our sleep was then disturbed only by such trifles as distant owlets, pariah dogs, jackals, brain-fever birds, and dust storms.

I was next sent to the hills, where the spotted owlets ceased from troubling. *Athene brama* is scattered all over India, and, indeed, over most parts of Southern

Asia, but it does not ascend the hills to any great height. If you would evade these birds without going to the uttermost parts of the earth, you must either flee to the hills or betake yourself to Ceylon.

Eighteen months of Himalayan breezes, direct from the snows, sufficiently restored my shattered constitution to enable me again to face the spotted owlets. This time I was sent to the "Garden of India." The owlets were, if possible, more numerous and more vociferous than they had been in the desert. I thoughtlessly rented a bungalow, of which the roof was composed of a double layer of tiles. This is a most excellent arrangement for warding off the heat of the sun, but it has the drawback of forming a nesting-place after the heart of the spotted owlet.

I do not know how many birds used to spend the day among the tiles; there may have been twenty of them, or there may have been two hundred. The worst of spotted owlets is, that they will all insist on speaking simultaneously. There will perhaps be five of them sitting in a row. Number one begins to chatter, then all the rest join in and try to shout the first man down, just as the "seven sisters" do. The result is the most dreadful uproar, and any one who did not know the birds would think that there was murder in progress.

As a matter of fact, this is how the owlets enjoy themselves. Englishmen take their pleasures sadly; spotted owlets take them noisily. It is as impossible as it is unnecessary to describe the cries of the spotted owlets. It must suffice that it is a superb blend of caterwauling and screeching in B flat. Our owlet friends in the roof used to remain comparatively quiet from 8 a.m. to 2 p.m. This was presumably their sleeping-time. From the latter hour spasmodic outbursts of screeching would be heard. About five o'clock the birds used to emerge.

The spotted owlet is the most diurnal of the strigidæ. He does not object to daylight in the least. Only yesterday morning, at about half-past seven, I saw one of these birds sitting on the stump of a defunct tree. Cunningham states that he saw a pair of them flying about, and quarrelling fiercely, over a glaring high road near Delhi, in the full blaze of the early afternoon of an April day, and when the hot wind was raging like the blast from an oven.

Owls are built for night work. They have very large eyes, long ears, and their plumage is so constituted that they can fly absolutely noiselessly. They are birds of prey, and have to hunt in the silence of night, when the hum of insects is still, and the noises of the day are hushed; hence the necessity of silent flight. Most owls lie low during the day; not so much because the sun hurts their eyes as on account of the rough handling they receive at the hands of the rest of the feathered folk. Birds are like boys at school, they set upon every strange individual which shows itself. Some owls sleep in trees; such find it very difficult to elude their pursuers if they once expose themselves. They have no haven of refuge to which they can flee. Not so with the spotted owlet. It has a lair in the shape of a hole to which it can retire when mobbed. Consequently, it

THE SPOTTED OWLET

is very bold, habitually venturing forth in daylight. Thus the other birds grow accustomed to it, and do not so often molest it.

During the day the spotted owlet is, of course, civil enough to the other birds of its acquaintance. At night, however, its manner changes. No sooner has the sun sunk below the horizon than it assumes a cock-of-the-walk air, and then makes no bones about punching the head of a king-crow, or any other bird which ought to be abed.

The spotted owl is a ludicrous little creature. One cannot look at it without laughing. The moment the bird notices that you are watching it, it crouches in the most ridiculous manner, glares at you, and then treats you to abuse of which the quality is such that it would do credit to any coster. When you begin to laugh, the bird flies away in a huff.

Athene brama lives chiefly on insects, but it will attack shrews, mice, lizards, and small birds. Sometimes an unusually bold owlet ventures inside the bungalow in order to hawk the moths attracted by the light.

The bird breeds in February or March, and lays its eggs in the hole of a tree or building. The eggs are white, as are those of almost every bird which nests in a dark place. Birds cannot count above two, so that if eggs which are laid in semi-darkness were not white, some of them might become separated from the main body without being noticed by the bird, and so fail to be hatched.

In India, as in England, owls are accounted birds of

evil omen. According to my friend B. Kaccoo Mal Manucha, Rai Bahadur (whose book, "The Hindu Home Life," should be read by all), "If you love a person who does not return your love, offer a dish of meat prepared with an owl's flesh, and as soon as it is tasted, he or she will be head over ears in love with you."

Listen to this, ye languishing maidens and love-sick swains, listen! How is it that ye are so sad when spotted owlets innumerable are living in your neighbourhood?

But, stay, let me not raise false hopes! Not only has the owl, like the proverbial hare, to be caught before he is cooked, but when the bird is cooked, it is necessary to induce the object of your affections to eat him. This may prove a difficult task in this age of sordid epicureanism; nevertheless, one can but try: it should, after all, be possible to cunningly disguise the flesh in a well-thought-out savoury.

Owl's flesh has yet another useful property, as any native will tell you. If a wife finds her husband intractable, if he persists in staying late at the club, losing money at bridge, and so is not at home at the dinner-hour, all the wife has to do is to give him boiled owl's flesh to eat, and he will, if he eats it, henceforth be as butter in his wife's hands.

But no rose is without its thorn. In spite of all the virtues inherent in the bird's flesh, you must "never allow an owl to rest on any portion of your building, as that means ruin to the inmates."

This must be true, because Kaccoo Mal says so; yet

dozens of owls have sat and squabbled on my double-tiled roof, and I have hitherto managed to avoid the bankruptcy court. I say this in no boasting spirit, but simply by way of encouragement to those who may one day chance to see, sitting on their roof, a spotted owlet.

THE SHAPES OF BIRDS

THE enormous and sudden advance made by zoological science in the latter half of the nineteenth century has been followed by a reaction. During the last ten or twelve years that particular branch of knowledge has made comparatively little progress. Darwin and Wallace completely revolutionized biology. They shed the light of the highest genius on the darkness which had hitherto brooded over the study of life. Their researches gave an enormous impetus to natural science. Nor were these the only stimuli. The theory of natural selection met at first with very bitter opposition on all sides. This opposition stirred up the Darwinians to new exertions.

Unfortunately the opposition was very shortlived. The triumph of the theory of natural selection was as speedy as it was complete. It would, I believe, have been more profitable to biological science had the conflict been of longer duration. Natural selection has won all along the line. It has proved itself able to explain a large number of phenomena, it has overcome a multitude of difficulties. Facts which were at one time urged against it are now held to be among the most powerful arguments in its favour. It is to-day almost universally accepted as a solution of all biological problems. It has come to be regarded with almost superstitious reverence as the master-key which is able to open the doors of all the passages which lead to the secret chambers of Nature. So great is our confidence in the powers of this master-key that we have even neglected to put it to the test in some cases. It has succeeded in very many instances, we therefore assume that it must be successful in all. It has unlocked the main doors, hence we deem it unnecessary to try it with smaller ones.

In other words, zoological science is in danger of stagnation. I admit that much useful work is being accomplished. Never before were so many workers in the field. A mass of new facts is accumulating. Daily, fresh contributions are added to our zoological knowledge. But each worker restricts himself to one small portion of the field, so that the main theory has made but little progress.

It is time that there was a fresh stocktaking; that the new facts discovered were co-ordinated, and their relations to one another and to the main theory studied. At present the tendency is to attribute almost supernatural powers to natural selection, to believe that it is the key to every biological problem.

If we ask why an animal is of such-and-such a colour, we are told natural selection has given the creature its colour as being that best suited to its needs. If we say that we fail to see how that particular colour is more useful to the animal than every other, we are told that as soon as we learn all the habits of the creature in question we shall see how perfectly its colour is adapted to its mode of life. This may be so. Nevertheless this kind of argument is not scientific. It tends to stifle inquiry, which is the true spirit of science.

The fact is that natural selection is a horse ridden to death. It is indisputably a most important factor in organic evolution, but are we justified in regarding it as the only factor? It is unable, I think, to explain many natural phenomena. One of these is the varying shapes of nearly allied animals.

Certain it is that the general form of a class of organisms is determined by natural selection, but are the thousand and one shapes seen among closely related creatures all to be explained by saying that were these of any other form they would perish in the struggle for existence?

Birds afford a striking example of the many shapes which may be assumed by creatures of very similar habits. I recently visited the Nilgiris, and spent many hours in a wood which might appropriately be called "The Flycatchers' Wood." No fewer than five species of that family are common in the wood of which the area is less than 5000 square yards. All these species have very similar habits.

To enumerate them. There is first the white-browed fantail flycatcher (*Rhipidura albifrontata*), a bird too well known to need detailed description. It will suffice that its chief characteristic is the tail, which it continually spreads out into a fan. This appendage is about three and a half inches long, that is to say, equal in length to the rest of the bird. Next comes the black and orange flycatcher (*Ochromela nigrirufa*), which looks for all the world like a robin. Its tail is only two inches long, while the body is three. Then there is the grey-headed flycatcher (*Culicicapa ceylonensis*). This, too, is a squat-figured little bird. The Nilgiri blue flycatcher (*Stoparola albicaudata*) next demands notice. In shape it differs from all the three birds mentioned above. Its tail is relatively short, and its body slim and elongated by comparison with the grey-headed and black and orange species. Moreover, it is sexually dimorphic. The male is indigo blue, while the female is brownish. There remains Tickell's blue flycatcher (*Cyornis tickelli*). This is a beautiful little bird, differing in shape from the birds already mentioned to such an extent that, quite apart from its distinctive plumage, it would be impossible to confound it with any of them. I did not see the paradise flycatcher (*Terpsiphone paradisi*), but the bird is found in the Nilgiris and probably visits the wood in question. The male of this species, when he comes of age, has a tail sixteen inches long; that is to say, four times the length of his body, while the tail of the hen bird makes up but half of her total length.

These birds, which display considerable variety as regards shape, have very similar habits. They all feed on insects, which, to quote Mr. Oates, they either catch on the wing, starting from a perch to which they usually return several times, or by running with the aid of their wings along the limbs of trees. I believe that of those the fantail species alone runs along the branches of trees. Mr. Oates adds, "they seldom or never descend to the ground."

This statement is not strictly true. I have repeatedly seen the fantail, the grey, and the black and orange species on the ground. But the point I desire to emphasise is that their methods of obtaining food are all very much the same. Were all the species of the same colour and shape, I think few observers would be able to distinguish one species from another, merely by watching their methods of securing food. Their varied nesting habits would, of course, serve to distinguish them.

Here, then, we have five species of birds, living side by side, under similar conditions and eating the same description of food, obtained by like methods, yet arrayed in totally different plumage and of varying form.

Passing over the differences in colouration, let us confine ourselves to configuration. Why are these birds not all of the same shape? They are related to one another; all are descendants of a common ancestor, and, as we have seen, their methods of obtaining food are not marked by any considerable differences; why, then, are they not all of one shape—the shape best suited to flycatching birds?

I do not think for a moment that it is possible successfully to maintain that the shape of each particular species is so important to it that, were the bird of any other shape, it must perish in the struggle for existence. The paradise flycatcher disproves such an hypothesis. The male and female differ considerably in form, yet both are equally successful in obtaining food, and both secure it in the same manner. Moreover, the young male has a tail four inches in length, but, later on, he grows one sixteen inches long, yet he continues to obtain food in the same manner. Thus a difference of twelve inches in the length of his tail does not appreciably affect his ability to find food.

Even if we could demonstrate that each species takes the shape best suited to its mode of life, if we could prove, for example, that the Nilgiri blue flycatcher would be greatly handicapped in the search for food were his shape that of the grey-headed flycatcher, this would not be sufficient. If natural selection alone is responsible for the shape of an organism, we must prove that every step in the transition from the common ancestral form to that of the present species was a distinct gain to the species. This point is often lost sight of by those who invoke the aid of natural selection to explain every zoological difficulty. It seems to me that the great diversity in shape exhibited by birds having similar habits merely shows that there are several equally good methods of accomplishing an object.

If Nature desires to call into existence a number of flycatching birds, she is not obliged to cast all in exactly the same mould; she is able to create many different forms of organism, all well adapted to the work before them. The general shape is of course determined by natural selection, especially in the case of highly specialized birds, such as woodpeckers, kingfishers, and swifts. But, even in such cases, considerable diversity of form is permitted. The less specialized the habits of a bird are, the greater is the latitude as regards shape allowed to it.

The shape of organisms is due to the action of a large number of forces, of most of which we are totally ignorant. Natural selection does not interfere unless the variation in shape tends to benefit or injuriously affect the possessor. In the former case, the beneficial shape tends to be perpetuated and to cause the species to spread at the expense of other less-favoured ones. In the latter case the injurious variation leads to the extermination of the creatures in which it appears.

Natural selection, like the stone walls of a labyrinth of lanes, marks certain limits within which variations as regards shape may persist. So long as the variations are such as do not affect the mobility of a species, its ability to obtain food, or its relationship to its environment, natural selection does not in any way interfere.

The causes which have produced this diversity of shape among allied species and genera have yet to be discovered. We are not at present in a position to say why some birds are large and others small, why some are slim and others stout, why some have pointed wings and others round ones, why some have broad heads and others narrow ones. It is useless to pretend that natural selection explains all these phenomena. It is better to be honest and frankly admit our ignorance.

WINGED FISHERFOLK

GREAT is the community of the winged fisherfolk, and varied are its methods of securing its prey! Madras, being well supplied with sheets of water, is largely patronized by our feathered fishing friends. The kingfishers—the most able exponents of the piscatorial art—have already received our attention ; we may, therefore, pass them over and proceed at once to study the ways of some of their professional brethren. Of these the osprey (*Pandion haliætus*) is, to my mind, *facile princeps.* There is, in nature, no finer spectacle than one of these great birds at work. Watch it as it makes its way high over the water, now flapping its broad pinions, now gliding as a kite does. Suddenly something below arrests its attention. It hovers for a second, its wings then close and it drops like a falling stone. It enters the water with a mighty splash, sending up showers of spray, and disappears for a moment. A second later it emerges, the water pouring off its back and wings, with a fish in its talons. It then betakes itself to some suitable place in which to devour its quarry.

The osprey is a winter visitor to India. It is abundant about the great backwaters of the east coast.

There must be half a dozen of these fishermen which carry on their trade in the Pulicat Lake. The backwater at Ennore has also its complement of these magnificent birds. Seen as it rests on a pile marking the channel of the canal through the shallow lake, the bird may be easily mistaken for a large kite, its length being six or seven inches more than that of the common kite. Its head, breast, and lower parts are, however, white. There is a broad black bar running down each side of its neck. The back and wings are dark brown. But it is by its habits rather than its appearance that one recognizes the osprey.

The fishing operations of the terns, or sea-swallows as they are sometimes called, fall rather flat after those of the raptorial bird. When a tern dives there is none of the mighty splash which marks the performance above described. The tern does its work so neatly that it enters the water with little more commotion than that made by a falling pebble. The tern is to the manner born. It comes of a long line of fisher-folk.

For myriads of generations its ancestors have dived after their finny prey. The osprey, or fish-hawk as it is often called, is, on the other hand, a bird of prey which has taken to fishing. It is, so to speak, an amateur; exceeding skilled, it is true, but nevertheless, by comparison with the sea-swallow, an amateur. One naturally expects to see a tern dive for its food, but to witness a great bird of prey tumble headlong into the water, like a falling boulder, takes one's breath away.

It is the great skill of the tern which causes its

TERN

performance to appear commonplace. What bird is there more graceful than the swallow of the sea? There is something truly fascinating about it as it sails through the air. The easy motion of its long wings puts me in mind of a perfectly trained racing eight paddling up to the starting-post before a race.

Terns resemble swallows in many respects. The former are, of course, larger and of lighter hue. There is a marked difference, too, in the mode of flight. If a tern reminds one of a rowing eight paddling along, the swallow resembles the eight racing at high pressure.

No one can fail to recognize a tern. If you see a slenderly-built bird of whitish tinge, with long swallow-like wings and a forked tail, a bird which sails along easily over water, sometimes diving for a fish, more frequently picking something off the surface of the water, you may set that bird down as a tern.

Three species are common about Madras. The most abundant is the gull-bird tern (*Sterna angelica*). This is the least beautiful of the terns, but albeit a handsome bird. It may be seen any day looking for its quarry over the Cooum. Its under parts are pure white, its beak and legs are black, and it has also some black, more in summer than in winter, about the head. Its tail is not very deeply forked.

A far more striking bird is the Caspian tern (*Hydroprogne caspia*). It is the largest of the terns, being twenty inches in length. By its size you may know it, also by its black head and coral-red bill.

The third of the common Madras terns is the black-bellied tern (*Sterna melanogaster*). This is a bird one frequently sees when out snipe-shooting, since it does not confine its operations to rivers; indeed, it is more partial to marshes and tanks. The breast and lower parts are black. The tail is deeply forked, hence this species is easily distinguishable from the other two common terns. It is a very elegant bird.

The transition from the tern to the gull is an easy one; so slight are the anatomical differences that some ornithologists look upon both groups as one family. The gull, however, is more stoutly built and flies differently. It is not so graceful. A gull looks best when riding on the water like a duck. It possesses great powers of flight, but is not the equal of the tern in this respect; its wings are smaller in proportion to the size of the body, hence gulls are often seen resting on the water, an attitude which terns rarely adopt, although their feet are webbed and admirably fitted to act as propellers.

Gulls are fond of fish, but they are inclined to be lazy. In preference to fishing for themselves they will follow a ship and pick up the scraps thrown overboard by the cook, or will hang about near a human fisherman for the sake of the fish rejected by him. Almost any day, half a dozen laughing-gulls may be seen in attendance on the fishermen of the Cooum, waiting for what these latter cast away, for there apparently exist aquatic creatures at which even a Cooum fisherman draws the line!

A number of crows usually keep the gulls company. There is consequently a great scramble for the leavings

BLACK-HEADED GULL.

of the net, stand-up fights sometimes taking place between "a lurking villain crow" and a gull over a tit-bit.

A number of gulls inhabit the Thames in London, and feed almost exclusively on the bread thrown to them by the passers-by. These gulls have now become quite an institution, and many clerks and other City men make a point of feeding them every day.

On the voyage to and from England gulls follow the steamer for the greater part of the journey. It is on these occasions that one is best able to realize the flying powers of a gull. The birds keep pace with a P. and O. steamer with ridiculous ease. A dozen flaps of the wing in a minute suffice to enable them to outdistance the ship.

The commonest gull in Madras is known to naturalists as the laughing-gull (*Larus ridibundus*). Why it is so called I have never been able to discover. It is difficult to describe this or any other gull in such a way as to render its identification an easy matter, unless, of course, the bird be held in the hand.

The laughing-gull may be distinguished from the brown-headed gull, which also visits Madras, by the fact that the wing of the former is the shorter by over an inch and its first quill is white, with black edges and tip, while in the latter species the quill is black, with a subterminal white band. To recognize a free bird in this way is about as easy as catching it by putting salt on its tail. Then, again, young gulls differ considerably in appearance from the adults. Lastly, most species are seasonally dimorphic; in winter the head is usually white, while in summer it becomes dark brown or black.

We must, in conclusion, consider a fishing bird of a very different type. I refer to the little cormorant (*Phalacrocorax javanicus*). This fowl, if not found actually within the limits of Madras city, is plentiful enough on the Red Hills tank and other sheets of water, fresh or salt, in the neighbourhood. The little cormorant is a duck-like bird of which "Eha" seems to entertain a very low opinion. "I dare say," he writes, "it often passes for a sort of black duck, but it differs from a duck as a gentleman differs from a loafer. The cormorant is a thoroughly shabby bird, with a large ragged tail, and coloured all over a sordid black, like the Sunday coat of a Goanese cook."

Here I am obliged to respectfully differ from "Eha." I consider the little cormorant a handsome bird, and as a swimmer or a diver it has no equal. It has the power of suddenly changing its specific gravity. One moment the bird is floating, cork-like, on the surface of the water, the next it is sinking like a stone. I once saw a wounded cormorant give three determined men half an hour's chase in water less than three feet deep. The bird had been shot to provide for the "inner men" of our boat coolies, so they rushed eagerly to seize their booty, but the bird, although wounded, had no intention of surrendering. Whenever a pursuer drew near, the cormorant dived and, thirty seconds or so later, reappeared at a distance of several yards. That cormorant must have dived thirty times before it was secured.

Had it not been made into a curry that night, the German Emperor would undoubtedly have sent it a telegram and probably decorated it. The sight of three men being repeatedly "scored off" by the bird would have been most ludicrous, had one not known that the poor creature was wounded and fighting for its life.

The little cormorant lives exclusively on fish, for which it dives. It is most voracious. I have never taken the trouble to count the number of fish put away by a cormorant in the course of a meal. One observer did, and saw the bird swallow 108 fish in the course of an hour and a half.

The heathen Chinee, with diabolical cuteness, makes the cormorant fish for him. He puts a rubber ring round the bird's neck, so that it cannot swallow its prey. It is, therefore, obliged to disgorge its booty into its master's basket. This is exploitation of labour if you like.

What a grand simile for the labour agitator! Just as a wicked Chinaman robs the poor cormorant of its earnings, so does the abominable capitalist exploit the working man. Therefore down with the bloated aristocracy, and let the honest worker enjoy twelve hours' play and twelve hours' sleep, and spend the remainder of the day in manly toil!

But this is a digression. It is only fair both to the cormorant and its master to say that the Chinaman now and then allows the bird to eat a fish, just to keep it in a good temper!

The meal over, the little cormorant betakes itself to

a post, upon which it squats with its wings partially expanded, looking like a church lectern.

Cormorants are very fond of perching on piles, from which they contemplate the world in solemn silence; in such an attitude they always put me in mind of the pillar saints of old.

THE UGLIEST BIRD IN THE WORLD

MEN may differ as to which is the most beautiful of the fowls of the air, but there can be no two opinions as to which is the ugliest bird in the world. This proud distinction, I submit, indubitably belongs to the white scavenger vulture (*Neophron ginginianus*), better known as "Pharaoh's chicken." Naturalists vie with one another in calling the creature names. "Eha" stigmatizes it as "that foul bird." Colonel Cunningham grows quite eloquent in his abuse of the *Neophron* tribe. According to him, they are "truly 'base and degrading' objects"; "any close acquaintance with them," he writes, "and specially a near view of them, as they wander about over heaps of rubbish in quest of their loathsome food, can only tend to arouse a sense of wonder that any birds should have succeeded in becoming so repulsive. St. Beuve, in writing of Talleyrand, affirms that "it takes a great deal of trouble to become wholly depraved," but *Neophrons* have certainly spared no effort to attain that end. Perhaps the question will be asked: "Why discourse upon this unlovely bird?"

Let me answer it in anticipation. Firstly, the creature

is, like Ally Sloper, a true friend of man. How we should get on without him in that land of primitive sanitation—India—I know not. Secondly, this vulture is, in South India, or, at any rate, in some parts of the Madras Presidency, a sacred bird.

The ancient Egyptians, also, seem to have held "His Riverence" in high esteem, for several portraits of the nearly allied Egyptian species are displayed in the museum of antiquities at Cairo.

Before dilating upon the virtues of the noble fowl it is necessary to describe it. The bird is delightfully easy to depict. There is no other creature like unto it. It is about the size of a kite. Its plumage is dirty white, except the tips of the wings, which are shabby black. The neck is covered with feathers, which stick out like the back hairs of a schoolboy. These are, if possible, rather dirtier-looking than the rest of the plumage, and frequently assume a rusty hue. Its bill is yellow, so are its naked face and its legs.

As "Eha" remarks: "It does not stand upright, like the true vultures, but carries its body like a duck and steps like a recruit."

There is told a story, which has by this time become quite a seasoned "chestnut," of a keen "griffin" going out with his gun on the day after his arrival at his first station in India. His bag for the day consisted of one *Neophron ginginianus*. This he sent, on the advice of a fellow-subaltern, to his Colonel's wife, with a polite note expressing the hope that she would accept the results of his first day's *shikar*. The inventor of this story might read with benefit a certain address de-

YOUNG SCAVENGER VULTURE IN NEST

livered by a certain Viceroy of India at a University not a thousand miles from Calcutta.

The scavenger vulture is found all over India; when, however, you come to the neighbourhood of Delhi his beak becomes less yellow and he grows larger. Needless to say that this is quite sufficient provocation for the manufacture of a new species.

The scavenger vulture of the Punjab is known as *Neophron perenopterus*. This multiplication of species is doubtless a very fine thing. But it makes things exceedingly unpleasant for the birds that live in the region where the races fuse with one another. These birds do not know what to call themselves: their bill is too yellow to allow their admission into the *perenopterus* clan, and too dusky for the *ginginianus* tribe to have anything to say to them. In such a case it would, I think, be as well to round off matters by creating a third species—*Neophron neither-one-thing-nor-the-other*.

Of the feeding habits of Pharaoh's chicken the less said the better. It eats filth of any and every kind, and is quite content to subsist upon food which the vultures proper reject as unfit for vulturine consumption. Mr. Finn puts the matter in a nutshell when he states that the bird is "appallingly accommodating of stomach."

Most vultures seek their food by soaring high above the earth, and thus commanding a wide expanse of country. When a vulture espies a carcass it at once wings its way earthward. Its neighbour, who is soaring at a distance of some miles, sees it depart, and follows it. The second bird's neighbour does likewise, so that there are, in quite a short time, half a dozen or more vultures feeding on the carcass, to say nothing of a rabble of crows. The scavenger vulture adopts a different procedure. There are in every town in the East certain places where its food is almost invariably to be found; these it visits in turn. It is a good flier, and when seen upon the wing looks quite a respectable fowl. The under parts of its wings appear pure white in the sunlight, and the black border gives them a finish.

The nest of the scavenger vulture is in keeping with the character of the bird. It is a mass of sticks, dirty rags, and other rubbish heaped together anyhow. It is sometimes placed on a stout forked bough of a large tree; more often it is to be found on a building.

For many years some of the Madras *Neophrons* have utilized the steeple of the Scotch kirk as their nursery. As soon as one pair of vultures has brought up its family, the site is seized by another couple; hence, during most of the cold weather a lady vulture is to be seen "sitting" high up in the steeple.

This species seems rarely to lay more than two eggs. Frequently, as in the illustration, one only is laid. The egg is the solitary beautiful thing connected with scavenger vultures. Its colour is dark red or crimson, richly blotched with russet. These hues, alas! wash off. The bird will have nothing to do with cleanliness in any shape or form; if you want to keep her eggs you must have them unwashed. Yet even this most degraded of birds is not without its virtues. The hen scavenger is a good mother. It takes a lot to make her leave the nest. The bird at the kirk allowed Captain Fayrer and

SCAVENGER VULTURE ON NEST

myself to come within a few feet of her and take a photograph. Mr. William Jesse states that upon one occasion, when he wanted to take the egg, the hen vulture refused to budge, and had to be poked off the nest with a stick. This behaviour is not altogether due to the maternal instinct; the bird is of a sluggish disposition, shows little fear of men, and is easily tamed. One of these fowls used to be kept as a pet in the Madras Museum; it recently died of paralysis.

The young scavengers, when they leave the nest, are sooty brown in colour, and in consequence are often taken for members of a different species. Then, gradually, white feathers show themselves, so that, after a time, the birds have a speckled appearance. Eventually they emerge resplendent in the adult plumage. Is this transition from dark to light the result of sexual selection? Can it be that the lady vulture has taste in dress; that dirty white is to her what the hues of a sunset sky are to human beings?

We have, in conclusion, to regard the fowl in its sacred aspect. The scavenger vulture is the last bird around which one would have expected to see the halo of sanctity, and I believe that I am right in saying that the Hindus do not regard all scavenger vultures as sacred, but merely a chosen few. These may be seen at Conjeeveram, in the Madras Presidency, by those who are not sinners. Those of us who are scathed by the wickedness of the world may see, hanging up in the Madras Museum, a photograph of the holy birds being fed by a Brahmin. These birds are said to be metamorphosed human beings. I forget their former names, nor do I remember the why and the wherefore of the punishment inflicted upon them by Siva. But what matters this? Are not dates and facts but the dry bones of history? Let us have the flesh and blood of myth and tradition and leave the dry bones to others.

We are told that the Conjeeveram vultures are very aged; to be, for once, exact, they are twenty or thirty hundred thousand years old—more or less; but their eyes are not dim, and they have the invaluable gift of feeling the presence of a sinner. When a sin-stained human being approaches the portals of the temple, they refuse to show themselves. This, taken in connexion with the fact that thousands of men have seen these sacred birds, says much for the moral condition of the Madras Presidency.

NOISY BIRDS

AN article on the subject of noisy birds recently appeared in the "Spectator." It is evident that the writer is not personally acquainted with India. Had he been, he would certainly have taken some of his examples of noisy fowls from the *avifauna* of this country. It is true that India can boast of no quiet bird so vociferous as the campanero or bell-bird of America, whose voice is said to carry for three miles, that being about the distance "which would be selected (by preference) by its auditors!" However, as generators of noise, hornbills are not very far behind the bell-bird. The flapping of the wings of that most extraordinary of birds—the Great Hornbill—can be heard a mile away, the sound resembling that made by a railway train. The voice of the bird, moreover, carries a distance of many furlongs.

The writer in the "Spectator" declares that England, although it cannot boast of many vociferous birds, has some "which can hold their own with all but the most strenuous voices of the bird population of other lands." As a matter of fact, there is only one such bird in England, and that is the corn-crake. Take away this from the British Isles, and there is no bird left nearly so noisy as a dozen of our commonest Indian birds—birds which haunt our gardens and housetops.

As a sound-producer the corn-crake (*Crex pratensis*) is worthy of all respect; it has a faculty of "getting on the nerves" in a manner that might excite jealousy even in the breast of the Indian brain-fever bird. The corn-crake, or land-rail, as it is often called, is a summer visitor to the British Isles; stragglers have been heard of in India, but the bird does not properly belong to *avifauna* of that country.

Upon arrival in England it takes up lodgings in a cornfield, one next to a house by preference. Every evening, as the shades of darkness steal o'er the land, the bird tunes up. It has but one note—a raucous, rasping "crake." The bird shouts "crake" a hundred times a minute without a break until sunrise. It is impossible to drive the bird from the field in which it has taken apartments; at least, all the attempts I have made failed miserably. Yet some of them were well planned out and marked with determination.

Upon one occasion, the whole of a large and indignant household turned out into the fields, and, having formed a line, attempted to drive the crake before it. As the line approached the middle of the field the bird became silent. We hoped that it was running away. Presently we heard behind us, "Crake, crake, crake!" Again and again, the line was formed and the field beaten, but all in vain. The crake always managed to get behind us. This behaviour is fully in accordance with the description of the habits of the bird given in books on ornithology: it rarely flies, and, if chased, sprints along the ground amid the corn and "never runs straight, but makes as many turnings as a hare." After tramping the fields for nearly an hour, the aforesaid household returned home with the poor satisfaction of having provided some amusement for the bird.

I am told that debating societies are often at their wits' ends to find subjects for debate which have not been discussed *ad nauseam.* If this be so, I would suggest as a new subject—"Which is the more deserving of the title 'Brain-fever Bird,' the Indian hawk-cuckoo or the corn-crake?" Anglo-Indians will, of course, plump for the Oriental bird, which certainly has in its favour one strong point: it names the disease it tries to give you. It shrieks: "Brain fever, *brain fever*, BRAIN FEVER," until you think its syrinx must burst! But which is the greater evil—a succession of series of *crescendo* notes or one continuous rasping sound?

The Indian bird is certainly assisted by the climate. It makes a noise only in the hot weather. It avoids the hills. It does not patronize the city of Madras, for the reason that the climate is rarely warm enough for it. It cannot sing to advantage when the thermometer stands at anything like 90° in the shade. Nay, in the Punjab, when the iced drinks hiss as they come into contact with the parched throat, is its ideal climate. But you can see and shoot a brain-fever bird, which is more than you can do to a corn-crake.

Take away the latter bird from the English team, and what have you left? A lamentable "tail" composed of rooks, magpies, and starlings. I do not take account of such birds as peewits and curlews, for these, although blessed with loud, penetrating voices, shun human habitations; they are denizens of lonely moors and fens, where any bird or man is at liberty to raise his voice to the uttermost without being dubbed "noisy." If the English team is sadly weakened by the absence of the corn-crake, the brain-fever bird is scarcely missed from the Indian eleven. His cousin, the koel (*Eudynamis honorata*), who is very partial to Madras, is an efficient substitute. Indeed, he is often called the brain-fever bird in this part of the world, but never by those who have listened to the real article. His *crescendo* "Kuil, kuil, kuil," heard both by day and by night, is a noise of which any fowl might be proud.

The white-breasted kingfisher is another noisy bird very common in Madras. His harsh scream is only too familiar to us. But we tolerate it for its beauty's sake. As he dashes through the air, with the sun shining on him, he is a truly magnificent object—a dazzling flash of blue, of which the brilliance is enhanced by a setting of chocolate and white.

In spite of his small size, the spotted owlet can hold his own, as regards vociferousness, against all comers. It is true that his caterwaulings cannot be heard three miles away. If they carried that distance the inhabitants of India would all be deaf mutes. In the vicinity of Madras there must be between six and seven hundred spotted owlets to the square mile, so that, if their voices were audible three miles away, and all spoke at once, we should spend our nights listening to a chorus of about two thousand spotted owlets.

The peacock is another Indian bird whose histrionic efforts "take a lot of beating." Like so many noisy birds, he prefers to raise his voice in the night time. His note resembles a loud, plaintive, very much drawn-out "miau," such as a lusty cat might emit. In some parts of India pea-fowl are accounted sacred birds and are often semi-domesticated, roosting in the trees near a village and feeding on the crops. When camping near such a village, for the first time, one is apt to pass a sleepless night, thanks to the pea-fowl, the jackals, and the village dogs.

The boisterous screams of those ruffians the "green parrots" are not often heard in Madras; nevertheless, these birds must be numbered among the noisy members of society. They are very numerous in many mofussil stations, while in the city of Bombay they are as abundant as mynas. The voice of the green parrot does not get on the nerves; it is, on the contrary, pleasant to the ear, being heard only for an instant as a flight of the birds dashes overhead upon felony intent. Of all the cultivator's enemies, the green parrot is the chief.

Another noisy bird, which is very common in most parts of India, but which, for some reason or other, avoids Madras, is the Indian magpie (*Dendrocitta rufa*). Although nearly related to the English magpie, this bird is of very different appearance, being dark brown with greyish wings and tail. This latter is over a foot in length. The Indian pie lives chiefly in trees. It goes about in small companies, which spend half the day in loudly squabbling among themselves and the other half in robbing birds' nests. The green barbets would take a prominent position among the noisy members of bird society in any country. Their note is loud, persistent, and penetrating; but they are not found in Madras itself. There their cousin, the coppersmith, replaces them. He is not nearly so noisy as they, but he is an untiring musician, and thinks it impossible to have too much of a good thing, when that good thing happens to be his own voice—a characteristic which he shares with some human beings.

Indian birds exist which have remarkably loud voices for their size, to wit, the ubiquitous tailor-bird and the iroa. These are so small that they would go comfortably into one's watch-pocket, yet their voices can be heard at a distance of two hundred yards or more. Were these birds as large as the great hornbill, and their voices increased in proportion, they would be formidable rivals of the American bell-bird. But they are not as big as hornbills, and we must take things as they are and not include them among our noisiest birds. They, however, deserve a place in the second rank, with the crows, the babblers, the black partridges, the king-crows, and the other minor poets.

INDIAN SONG-BIRDS

HAVING discoursed upon the noisy birds of India, it is but fitting that we should give the songsters an innings, for we have some song-birds in the East, notwithstanding the article of the Anglo-Indian creed, which declares that in the country of his adoption birds do not sing, that they caw, croak, squeak, and make all manner of objectionable and abominable noises, but sing—no! This article of belief is a gross libel on many birds. Nevertheless, those who subscribe to it are able to plead extenuating circumstances, for, as we have seen, India is the happy hunting ground of a whole army of noisy birds, many of which are exceedingly abundant, and not only exasperate the European beyond measure by their importunity, but drown the melody of those birds which have tuneful voices.

> "The nightingale, if she should sing by day
> When every goose is cackling, would be thought
> No better musician than the wren."

India possesses some song-birds which can hold their own against all comers. This any unprejudiced observer will admit. The Englishman is, of course, not an unprejudiced observer. It is impossible to bring him to believe that the song of any foreign bird can equal the avine melodies of the homeland; and from his point of view he is undoubtedly right. Here in India the associations are wanting which endear to him the voices of the feathered folk at home. Yet a real live nightingale sometimes visits India. It is true that the melodious bird does not venture far into that uninviting land. Nevertheless the Persian nightingale (*Daulias golzi*) does pay parts of the Punjab a visit in the cold weather. Many are taken to Calcutta in captivity. Since a good specimen will fetch as much as Rs.200 in the Calcutta market, it is not surprising that some men make it their profession, and a cruel profession it is, to catch, imprison, and then send these birds to the city by the Hooghly.

Of the permanent residents in India, the shama (*Cittocincla macrura*) is perhaps the finest singer. This bird is not likely to be heard in any large town. It loveth not the unseemly din of the city. It lives among shady hills, and, if we would hear its splendid voice in its full magnificence, we must betake ourselves to one or other of the great forests of India. A fine songster, nearly related to the shama, and which is found in nearly all parts of India, is the magpie robin or dhyal (*Copsychus saularis*). This is a charming creature, having the confiding habits of the robin, the bright colouring of the magpie, and the voice of the canary. It is nearly always found near human habitations. It is essentially a garden bird, nesting in holes in trees, or buildings. I once found a magpie robin's nest in the dilapidated wall of a stable. It generally breeds from April to July.

I am ashamed to say that I had known the bird for a long time before I became acquainted with its song. One day, my work detained me late, so, instead of going to club as usual, I took a stroll in the garden; my progress was soon arrested by an exceptionally fine song, of considerable power and great compass: on looking up, I discovered, to my great surprise, that the vocalist was a common magpie robin which was sitting on a bare branch. Since that day I have listened to its voice so frequently that it is a mystery to me that I had never heard it before.

How is it possible to explain this want of knowledge of the song of the common birds of India? Of course, the human ear is a strange organ. It continually receives thousands of vibrations, capable of being perceived as sound by the brain, which are never heard at all, sounds which, so to speak, pass in at one ear and out of the other. Soft sounds seem never to be perceived unless the ear is consciously or unconsciously listening for them.

In the early morning and late afternoon, when most of the Indian birds pour forth their song, the ear is greeted by myriads of sounds, many sharp and powerful, so that the soft musical ones, which do not grate upon the auditory nerve, are apt to pass unnoticed.

Then one walks so little in India. When driving, the rumbling sound of the carriage wheels drowns, to a great extent, the songs of the smaller birds; under such circumstances, these can be heard by listening for them, and, in order to listen for a sound, one has to know it. If we in India could only indulge in country walks as we do in our own land, we should soon learn to recognize and to love the tunes of the commoner singing birds. But alas! a country walk in India without grassy downs, gay hedgerows and leafy glades, is apt to have a depressing effect on the exiled European, so he takes his exercise in the form of games.

The plumage of the cock dhyal is glossy black, except the breast, abdomen, and sides of the tail, which are white. The bird is also marked by a broad white band on each wing, seen when the latter is closed. The animal has, therefore, a smart appearance; it is always spick-and-span, and struts about in a most sprightly manner; its jaunty air is heightened by the fact that the tail is carried erect. In the female the black of the plumage is replaced by a slaty colour.

The magpie robin will live in captivity; it, however, is not often seen as a caged bird, for its cousin, the shama, having a more beautiful song, is more highly esteemed. The dhyal spends a good deal of its time in trees, as often as not among the bare branches, so that it is always easy to see. From such a position it will pour forth its song in one continuous stream. Its notes are bright and joyous; they exhibit great compass and variety, while the volume of sound emitted is considerable for so small a bird, yet the bird just misses being a really great singer. Its notes are not marked by that absolute purity which constitutes so much of the beauty of the song of the nightingale, nor is its voice so mellow or sympathetic as that of the blackbird.

The magpie robin, like many great human singers,

pours forth its song in a *blasé*, unfeeling sort of way, and thus reveals its own character, for it is a solitary bird; the male is but rarely seen about with his wife. As Mr. Hudson has pointed out, the charm of the song of some birds—as, for instance, that of the willow wren—consists in the very human character of their notes, a feature which makes their song sink deep into one's heart. There is but little of this in the voice of the magpie robin, but, for all that, he is no mean singer and daily pours forth his beautiful notes, which fall on the dull senses of the stolid native or the unhearing ears of the indifferent European.

No account of the songsters of India would be complete which did not notice the dainty pied wagtail—the most charming of birds, which nests about our houses and gladdens them with the soft, sweet song, which it pours forth at all seasons of the year.

The Indian robin is another of our singing birds. It is found all over India; but robins south of the Godaveri River differ slightly from those which dwell in Northern India. Hence ornithologists recognize two distinct species of Indian robin. It is not a difficult bird to recognize, being quite a robin in build and habits. It differs from the robin we know in England in wearing, instead of a red waistcoat, a red seat to its trousers. The cock bird is blackish and the hen brownish; both have a narrow white bar in the wing. It hops about the garden in a very familiar way, just as the English robin does. It nests in all manner of queer places, in a hole under the thatch, in the midst of a pile of stones, or in a cranny in a wall. The nest is not easy to find, for the bird absolutely refuses to enter when it knows that any one is watching it.

Some time back, when walking in a suburb of Madras, I was stepping over a low prickly-pear bush, when two young robins fluttered out, almost from under my feet. They could scarcely fly, so young were they, consequently I am sure they came out of a nest, and that the nest was somewhere under the prickly-pear. Nevertheless, half an hour's search was not sufficient to reveal the nest, which must have been in the midst of the bush, and prickly-pears demand respectful treatment. All the while I was poking about for the little nursery the parent birds sat on branches near by and swore at me. But when, eventually, I had to admit defeat and depart without having set eyes on the nest, the notes of anger were speedily replaced by little songs of joy.

The Indian skylark must be recognized as one of the chief of our esteemed singing-birds, since its song is in no way inferior to that of its cousin found in England. We do not hear much of the Indian bird because the crows never give it a chance. Their rowdy noises drown the skylark's song.

A more vociferous singer and one which it would take a whole army of crows to swamp is the white-browed fantail flycatcher (*Rhipidura albifrontata*). This sprightly bird has a loud and cheerful song of six or seven notes: these, says Mr. Ferguson, remind one of the first bars of the "Guards' Valse."

The golden oriole is one of the few birds which have the twofold gift of a melodious voice and beautiful

THE INDIAN ROBIN

plumage. Dame Nature is inclined to be parsimonious. If she arrays a bird in very handsome clothes, she is usually content to allow it but a poor song. In the same way, most of the birds which are endowed with sweet voices are plainly attired. She has, however, been very generous to the oriole. She has lavished upon it with no unsparing hand the most brilliant yellow and golden tints to be found in her paint-box, and, in addition, has taught the bird to utter a note very agreeable to human ears. The mellow *peeho, peeho*, or *loriot, loriot*, as the French syllabize the note, is perhaps the most pleasing of the sounds which issue from the mango tope.

The Malabar whistling thrush (*Myiophonus horsfieldii*), commonly known as "the idle schoolboy," is one of the most characteristic song-birds of Southern India. But he does not visit Madras; his haunts are "far from the madding crowd." He is abundant on the West Coast. I do not know what constitutes his eastern boundary, but probably he does not occur east of the Shevaroy Hills. He is seldom found far from water. He loves to whistle his merry tune to the accompaniment of running streams. "Few birds," writes Eha, "have been endowed with so rich a voice, and it would be world-famous as a songster if it could only learn a tune. It is always practising, but makes no progress." It commences to whistle a cheery lay and then suddenly stops short; it is this habit which has earned for it the name of "the idle schoolboy."

The Bhimraj or larger racket-tailed drongo (*Dissemurus paradiseus*) deserves a place of honour among the song-birds of India. According to Mr. Oates, this drongo "has a really fine song, and is perhaps the best singing-bird of the East." This statement should, however, be accepted with reserve, for, in my opinion, Mr. Oates is not a first-class judge of the quality of a bird's song. He speaks of the magpie robin as only "a fairly good songster." After this one is surprised at no opinion of his regarding the vocal powers of a bird. The truth of the matter is that the Bhimraj, which is just a glorified king-crow—one having a crest and a tail twenty inches long—is a perfect mimic. According to Jerdon, it will "imitate all sorts of sounds, as of dogs, sheep, cats, goats, poultry, and the notes of many birds; hence it used to be called by some *Hazar-dastan*, or the bird with a thousand tales (not tails). Blythe had one that imitated the fine song of the shama to perfection." The Bhimraj makes an excellent pet.

There are in India, as in every country, a whole host of birds which perhaps scarcely merit the name of song-birds, but which, nevertheless, emit very pleasant sounds; such are the bulbuls, mynas, bee-eaters, and king-crows. None of these are very great musicians, but we should be sorry to lose their voices. Were there no bulbuls our hill stations would lose half their charm, and were the mynas and the king-crows to disappear the plains of India would become very dreary.

It is probably quite incorrect to include the cuckoo among the song-birds. Nevertheless I am going to do so, for the simple reason that there are few birds of which the note is more pleasing to my ear. I have no sympathy with the cross-grained old poet who spoke of the "leud Cuckoo" and said, "I pray to God will fire her bren." Rather would I cry with Wordsworth—

> "O Cuckoo! shall I call thee bird?
> Or but a wandering voice?
>
> . . . .
>
> Darling of the spring.
> No bird: but an invisible thing—
> A voice or mystery."

The European cuckoo visits India. I have never heard it in the south of the peninsula, but others have been more fortunate. From April to June the Himalayas resound with its familiar call. The bird is there, as in England, the harbinger of spring. A Himalayan station in springtime is a sight for the gods. It is a parti-coloured island cast in a magenta sea, for the rhododendrons are in bloom. The spiræa hedgerows have felt the touch of spring; their snowy flowers have come forth in such abundance as to obliterate the foliage. The horse-chestnut trees have awakened from their long winter sleep; they have opened out their emerald fans, and over these profuse Nature has showered "ten thousand waxen pyramidal flowers." Here and there a mass of the pale yellow blossom of the mimosa trees forms a pleasant contrast to the deeper tints of the horse-chestnut inflorescences.

The little hill gardens are gay with English flowers: roses, carnations, honeysuckle, geraniums, phlox, portulacas, nasturtiums, and sweet peas vie with one another for supremacy, and turn the flower-beds into patches of brilliant colour. In the far distance the great snow-clad mountains watch over all. When the cuckoo pours forth his "sovereign cry" amid such surroundings, one feels that it is good to live and that there is no song equal to that of the cuckoo; but perhaps the truth of the matter is contained in the lines—

> "Not in thy double note the magic lies,
> But in the fields and woods, the streams and skies."

GLOSSARY

Bagh. Grove or garden planted with trees.

Chapatti. A thin, flat cake made of unleavened bread, and commonly eaten by the natives of Northern India.

Chaprassi. Lit. a badge-man. A servant who runs messages.

Chik. A number of thin pieces of bamboo strung together to form a curtain. *Chiks* are usually hung in front of doors and windows in India with the object of keeping out insects, but not air.

Chota haziri. Early morning tea.

Dâk. Post.

Dâk bungalow. Government rest-house. Sometimes a cook is attached to the dâk bungalow, and he caters for visitors if they wish.

Dhobi. A washerman.

Dirzie. A tailor.

Durga Puja. A religious festival observed by the Hindus of Bengal.

Jhil. A lake, broad tank, or any natural depression which is filled with rain-water at certain seasons.

Kuch ne. Lit. "nothing." A term applied by native beaters to all non-game birds seen when one is out shooting.

Kunkur. Lumps of limestone with which roads are metalled in Northern India.

Machan. A platform erected in a tree, upon which the sportsman sits while waiting for his quarry.

Maidan. A flat, open space.

Mali. Gardener.

Mofussil. The outlying parts of a province as opposed to headquarters.

Murghi. Fowl.

Poochee. Insect.

Raj. Government.

Ryot or *rayat.* Husbandman, cultivator.

Shikar. Hunting or shooting.

Shikari. (1) The man who goes hunting or shooting.
(2) The native who accompanies him and directs the beat.

Topi or *toper.* Sun-helmet.

Usar. Land on which a saline deposit has formed.

BULBUL (RED VENTED)

RED WHISKERED BULBUL.

INDEX